HAUNTED
LINCOLN

HAUNTED
LINCOLN

DAVID BRANDON

First published 2009

The History Press
The Mill, Brimscombe Port
Stroud, Gloucestershire, GL5 2QG
www.thehistorypress.co.uk

Reprinted 2011

British Library Cataloguing in Publication Data.
A catalogue record for this book is available from the British Library.

ISBN 978 0 7524 4891 6

Typesetting and origination by The History Press
Printed in Great Britain by Marston Book Services Limited, Oxford.

CONTENTS

ACKNOWLEDGEMENTS

The ghostly and other associated phenomena described in this book come from a variety of sources, including many residents of Lincoln and Lincolnshire who have been kind enough to contact me about their experiences. To all of them I offer sincere thanks and I have in all cases maintained the anonymity which we agreed was desirable. I would like to thank the staff of the Lincoln City Library for their generous help. My son, Ed Brandon, took the photographs in Lincoln and its immediate area and acted as both a wise and a congenial companion and adviser throughout the project, as indeed he has before on other publications. His website is www.anotherstateofmind.co.uk. My thanks go to him. Alan Brooke, with whom I have collaborated on the writing of many books, took the pictures in Lincoln's rural hinterland and his help was greatly appreciated.

One

INTRODUCTION –
A SHORT AND SELECTIVE
HISTORY OF LINCOLN

Uphill Lincoln stands on a long ridge of Jurassic limestone overlooking the more workaday Lincoln down the hill. The lower part of the city stands on the plain of the River Witham which, having flowed northwards along the edge of the ridge, makes its way through the Lincoln Gap and flows off in a south-easterly direction towards Boston and the Wash. The position of Lincoln at this gap in the upland terrain close to the Witham made it a natural and early focal point of economic activity, communications, and administrative and military considerations. It was not far from the lowest bridging point on the River Trent and not far from the Humber, which provided access to and from vast swathes of midland and northern England. The Roman appreciation of the importance of the Trent is demonstrated by their building of the Fossdyke which linked the colony at what is now Lincoln and the Witham to the Trent at Torksey. As early as AD 47 the Romans had begun developing a fortress at the intersection of two great roads, Ermine Street from the south to the Humber and the Fosse Way south-westwards towards Bath. This fortress was to be occupied for upwards of 350 years. Many traces exist both of this military installation and of its dependent settlement or *colonia* and these have given rise to some of the ghost stories found in Lincoln and its surrounding area.

Lindum Colonia developed into one of the most important urban centres of Roman Britain. It was roughly rectangular in shape and covered an area from the Newport Arch down the hill almost as far as the Witham. It was contained within walls with some minor suburban settlement beyond, even on the other side of the Witham. As might be expected of the Roman colonists, an impressive range of amenities were provided to make life tolerable in this far-flung and, if truth be told, cold, damp and wearisome part of their empire. The story of the decline and eventual fall of this empire has been frequently told, but by the time the last military forces were withdrawn, hoards of fierce and barbarous invaders from northern Europe were ranging, largely at will, across much of what is now the East Midlands and Lincolnshire. These barbarians soon put down roots by settling there. These folk, conveniently categorized as Anglo-Saxons, seem to have had little time for towns and little sympathy with the partially-Romanized native population. It is likely that Lincoln was plundered, pillaged and put to the sword and the town went into serious decline after the Romans had left the locals to fend for themselves.

Then follows a period during which there is little recorded historical development, an era which used to be described misleadingly as the 'Dark Ages', as if it was nothing better than a black hole in the story of the people of these islands. The reality, of course, was that progress continued but within a culture very different from that which the Romans created. It is likely that conversion of the local population to Christianity took place in the seventh century because archaeologists have unearthed the remains of a simple church of that period. Under the Anglo-Saxons, Lincoln became part of the Kingdom of Mercia. In the second half of the ninth century, the district was despoiled by new raiders, this time the Danes who were intrepid mariners, warriors and explorers and they used the Trent as a convenient means to overrun the East Midlands. They worshipped Pagan gods and saw Christian places of worship – and the Christians themselves – as fair game. The Danes in turn began to settle in this part of England, particularly after the great English King Alfred came to an accommodation with them, a wise piece of political expediency known as 'the Danelaw'. Lincoln obviously struck a chord with the Danes who made Lincoln the foremost of the five boroughs which composed the Danelaw. Street names like Saltergate, Danesgate and Hungate bear witness to the time of their dominance. In due course, the Danes converted to Christianity and went native; the revived Anglo-Saxons wrested control back from them in AD 920. The times were still volatile and Lincoln probably found itself caught between the largely Anglo-Saxon dominated south of England and the north of England where the Norsemen held sway. This may have meant that Lincoln took on some of the cosmopolitan character of a frontier town. No real opportunity to develop much social and political stability was possible before yet another invading force arrived. These were the Normans, of course, and their arrival and conquest of the country was to bring about a much more thoroughgoing change in the economic, social and political nature of English society. Before 1066, however, the growing commercial and administrative importance of Lincoln is suggested by the development of a market and also a mint. The splendid towers of the churches of St Mary le Wigford and St Peter at Gowts suggest that despite the volatile political conditions of the late Saxon period, Lincoln was growing in prosperity. It is significant that they were built outside the town walls.

The Normans were great practitioners of *realpolitik* and were ruthlessly determined that the native population should be left in absolutely no doubt as to who was now in charge. Under their rule, Lincoln became one of the most important cities in the kingdom, and to symbolize their military and political control they built a castle on the dominant hill overlooking the Witham. It was blatantly obvious to everyone who was the king of the castle, and this assertive statement of the new reality was given spiritual and ideological backing in the erection of a cathedral within a few yards of the castle by the Norman bishop, Remigius. The castle was used as the headquarters of the sheriff with a court and armed support to look after the shire of Lincoln. The Bishop of Lincoln in turn looked after, at least in theory, the spiritual welfare of people in an enormous diocese stretching down as far as Dorchester-on-Thames. The establishment of Lincoln as the seat of the diocese led to the appearance of an army of clergy, bureaucrats, servants, stonemasons and other artisans, with their associated buildings, and their presence brought trade and business to the city. Lincoln also became famous as a centre of the wool trade.

Lincoln was to witness historical events of major importance over the following centuries. The twelfth century saw a great earthquake, several fires and destruction during the anarchic years in which the ineffectual Stephen slugged it out with the Empress Matilda for the crown of England. Henry II gave Lincoln several charters and, just for good measure, had himself crowned for the second time close to the city boundary, this being in the year 1157.

A prominent citizen of Lincoln during the reign of Henry II was Aaron the Jew, reputedly the richest man in England and the country's most successful moneylender. He frequently bankrolled the King and he provided finance for the construction of no less than nine Cistercian monasteries in England. His monetary resources came to the assistance of the cathedral on a number of occasions. Aaron died in 1186, he and other Jews having been taxed heavily but receiving useful civil privileges during the reign of Henry. Few people like moneylenders and the success of his financial transactions excited a great deal of jealousy and animosity. This hostility extended to the sizeable Jewish communities in Lincoln and elsewhere, and set the scene for an appalling outburst of racial hatred which besmirches the history of Lincoln.

Henry had been succeeded by Richard I, whose main purpose in life seemed to be the pursuit of plunder and ethnic cleansing under the guise of 'holy war'. To justify his aggression, he claimed the support of God in taking the offensive against all infidels, be they Muslims or, by implication, Jews. Two generations of religious persecution were to follow. Pogroms leading to massacres took place in 1189 in York and Norwich, but Lincoln's Jewish community had received warnings and they took refuge in the castle. This affair blew over but seeds had been sown and a more serious display of anti-Semitism occurred in Lincoln in 1255. The sizeable local Jewish community had been temporarily enlarged by many others who had arrived in the city for a wedding. The day after the ceremony, the dead body of a young gentile boy called Hugh, missing for three weeks, was found in a cesspit near the house belonging to a local Jew called Copin. Hugh's body was carried to the cathedral and buried near the tomb of Bishop Grosseteste. Immediately the idea was put around that Hugh was a Christian 'martyr' who had been put to death ritually by members of the wealthy Jewish community in the city. About twenty prominent Lincoln Jews were hanged and many others thrown into prison, only obtaining their release on the payment of substantial fines. The boy Hugh afterwards became known as 'Little St Hugh'; a shrine was erected and all sorts of miracles were alleged to have been performed by his remains. This came in handy as large numbers of pilgrims made their way to Lincoln, offering money at the shrine as evidence of their devotion and paying for food and accommodation in the city. Anti-Jewish feeling, incidentally, culminated with their expulsion from the kingdom in 1290.

It was at Lincoln in 1200 that King John received the homage of William of Scotland and in the same year, John was a pall-bearer when the body of Bishop Hugh of Avalon was carried in solemn procession to the west door of his cathedral. This particular Hugh (c. 1140-1200) is one of the major figures in the history of Lincoln. French by birth, he became a Carthusian monk and, by hard work and ability, caught the eye of those in power. He rebuilt the cathedral after the earthquake – although some say its collapse had been due to poor construction work – and he made Lincoln into what would now be described as a 'centre of excellence' in scholarship, administration and pastoral care. He was canonized and a shrine containing his relics was built for him in the cathedral. The shrine attracted large numbers of pilgrims and, as was usual with such items, the relics proved to be a great source of funds. Hugh never went anywhere without his pet swan – they were greatly attached to each other and he is always presented in iconography with the swan. Another great thirteenth-century bishop was Robert Grosseteste, likewise a notable scholar but with a tendency to be outspoken and critical of the Pope and the King. It is hardly surprising therefore that attempts to have him canonized were unsuccessful.

In 1280 Edward I and his beloved Queen Eleanor were present at the great pomp and ceremony which accompanied the relocation of the saintly Hugh's remains to its new shrine. Eleanor was in Lincoln again in 1290, but unfortunately this time she was a cadaver being carried through the city on the first stage of her journey from Harby in Nottinghamshire to burial at Westminster.

In 1301, Edward I was in Lincoln when he rather daringly issued a bold declaration to what passed for a Parliament at that time as he unequivocally told the Pope that he had no claim to sovereign powers over Scotland. In 1316, Parliament met in Lincoln again and raised money to supply Edward II with the resources for war against Scotland. In 1387, Richard II visited Lincoln and granted the mayor the right to have a sword carried before him in civic processions. Generally, however, the city was in the doldrums in much of the fourteenth, fifteenth and sixteenth centuries. Local government was feeble and corrupt, the woollen industry was stagnating and the Fossdyke was becoming difficult to navigate through lack of maintenance. Lincoln was finding itself off the beaten track as most road traffic to and from London, the north and Scotland was travelling to the west, up the Great North Road through Grantham and Newark. Worse was to follow, with outbreaks of the Black Death in 1349, 1361, 1369 and 1374. These outbreaks not only caused widespread premature death, but had disastrous economic and social effects, although not of course unique to Lincoln. Much of the city was described as 'ruinous' in the 1520s.

In 1485, Henry VII entered the cathedral and rendered thanks to the Almighty for his victory at Bosworth – some years later, Henry VIII and Catherine Howard enjoyed sumptuous hospitality at the Bishop's Palace. As part of the so-called Pilgrimage of Grace in 1536, anti-Royalist rebels stormed and destroyed the Bishop's Palace. The insurgents included the heads of a number of monasteries who paid for their defiance with their lives. Henry's religious reforms continued, in the course of which the cathedral was relieved of many of its precious possessions and sources of income such as its numerous chantries. In the seventeenth century, much of the cathedral fabric was in dire condition.

In 1617, James I spent several days in Lincoln. He was a curious man, a sophisticated intellectual in many respects who wrote a biting polemic against the practice of smoking and who could be a charming and stimulating companion. On this occasion, however, he preferred to spend his time in activities of a not particularly cerebral nature. These included cockfighting and hunting, where he surprised those who had not previously hunted with him. When the kill was brought to him, he climbed off his horse and sat down on the still warm carcass, smearing himself all over with blood. This, apparently, was his normal practice. At the start of the Civil War, Lincoln found itself at the centre of hostilities and was won and lost by Parliamentary forces before finally being taken from the Royalists by the Earl of Manchester's army in 1644. Manchester's men gave vent to their spleen by sacking the city, or at least those parts that had not previously been despoiled. Many scores continued to be settled even after the war was officially over and the mutual enmities among eminent local people that resulted from civil war and religious differences took centuries to eradicate. Plunder, pillage and disruption of trade had harmful effects on the local economy. The dour and unpopular Dutchman, William III, visited the city in 1695 when on his way to Welbeck in Nottinghamshire. This wasn't all bad, as he granted Lincoln the valuable right to have a new annual fair for livestock and general merchandise.

Lincoln entered the eighteenth century with its buildings, its local administration, its communications system and its economy in a very tumbledown condition. Lincoln's prosperity was always dependent on that of the agricultural countryside with which it was surrounded. Improvements in water and road transport, and investment by landlords in enclosures and more scientific and technological methods of farming effected a slow but definite change in the local economy during the century. Significantly, the population began to grow, reaching about 7,000 by 1800. County Assembly Rooms were built and the city, as befitting a county town, became the centre of Lincolnshire's prestigious social scene, especially when the races and the assizes were being held. Overall, prosperity increased but the growing wealth was shared out extremely inequitably. As it moved into the nineteenth century, Lincoln had large numbers of people in abject poverty living in accommodation that was often inferior to that in which the gentry housed their horses.

The late eighteenth and the nineteenth centuries witnessed the changes associated with the Industrial Revolution. Not least of these was the creation of national and international business, banking and trading links which meant that events hundreds or even thousands of miles away could have devastating effects on local economies. While the century saw impressive agricultural, industrial and commercial development, the process was punctuated by periodic slumps and depressions which could cause severe economic disruption and distress, at least in the short term. Improved local government services became available and early, faltering steps were taken to improve Lincoln's public health and environmental conditions and address other social issues, sometimes under local permissive initiatives and, on other occasions, as the result of mandatory national legislation.

Despite being the centre of a huge rural and agricultural hinterland, Lincoln in the nineteenth century developed as a very important industrial city, admittedly at first in activities which strongly reflected local farming activities. Iron founding became a major occupation, making pipes for drainage purposes and steam engines to carry out all kinds of labour-saving tasks on farms. The best-known firms in this business were Clayton and Shuttleworth, who were busily exporting agricultural machines across the world by the mid-1840s, and Rustons, who can trace their origins back to 1856. Malting, brewing, flour-milling, fertilizers and cattle-cake industries both drew on and, in turn, benefited agriculture locally and further afield. A complex network of railways opened up from 1846 and played a crucial role in bringing fuel and raw materials into Lincoln and transporting finished products away. However, it would be true to say that Lincoln suffered from not standing along the route of any of Britain's major trunk railway routes.

Rarely has any political constituency been served by a more colourful character than the man who became Lincoln's MP in 1826. He was a forty-three-year-old retired Army colonel of some distinction who belonged to a well-known Lincolnshire family and rejoiced in the name of Charles de Laet Waldo Sibthorp. Rarely, even among Tory backwoodsmen, can there have been such a glorious eccentric and hidebound reactionary as this little strutting coxcomb of a man. He set new standards of political and social reaction, nationalism and xenophobia which meant that whenever he arose to address the House of Commons, the MPs left the bars faster than if someone had shouted 'Fire!' He opposed just about any suggested innovation and reform, no matter how mild, and would inveigh against such proposals with a stream of forceful invective and splenetic venom which more than made up for the sheer illogicality of the speech and the fact that it was peppered with innumerable, totally irrelevant asides. He waxed angrier and more vehement the longer he spoke, he lacked even the merest smidgen of humour and dressed in a most dapper manner, albeit sporting fashions that had gone out of style fifty years earlier. His speeches brought the house down and found many of his colleagues rolling around in nearly terminal fits of laughter, tears coursing down their faces as they suffered the exquisite agonies of the stomach cramps brought on as the result of listening to Sibthorp's oratorical efforts. Anything he opposed was dismissed by him as a 'humbug', and there were few humbugs in his opinion worse than railways. With a steadfastness worthy of Horatius defending the bridge over the Tiber, Sibthorp became what we would now call a 'national treasure', admired for his entertainment value by political friend and foe alike. He was admired too by the admittedly small electorate of the city who, with only one brief lapse, elected him as one of their MPs right through till his death.

In the twentieth century, Lincoln grew considerably and had a population of more than 60,000 in 1911. A prominent local firm was William Foster, established in the previous century. This company, originally engaged in flour-milling, moved into the manufacture of agricultural machinery such as tractors. Some were designed with caterpillar tracks for moving across very difficult terrain. In 1915 the company was asked, as a matter of urgency, to adapt the caterpillar track idea for use on an armoured fighting vehicle. From these beginnings developed the tank, and the prototype of this revolutionary vehicle was tested at Foster's factory. Imagine the amazement and terror on the faces of the German soldiers dug into their trenches on the Western Front when these behemoths emerge from the early morning mist and lumbered, apparently inexorably, across No Man's Land and straight for their lines, peppering them with a deadly rain of cannonfire as they came! Ruston's, for their part, built large numbers of military aircraft, including the famous Sopwith Camel.

Lincoln became an important administrative and retail focus for its region, while its dependence on agriculture declined, as did its role as a manufacturing centre. Tourism became an important element in the local economy, now dominated by the provision of services rather than the making of things or, as some people might say, the creation of 'real wealth'. It is difficult to manage a balance between preservation and innovation, but Lincoln has come into the twenty-first century a lively, bustling city. It has undoubtedly benefited from the development and growth of higher education facilities and the emergence of a vibrant youth culture. The population is now over 90,000.

Two

GHOSTS AND OTHER SPOOKY SPECTRES

Millions of spiritual Creatures walk the Earth
Unseen, both when we wake, and when we sleep.

John Milton, *Paradise Lost: Book IV*

The ultimate mystery of life is what happens to us when we die. Is the soul, that vital spark that makes each of us distinctive individuals, simply snuffed out, followed rapidly by the decay of our physical parts? Most of us are inevitably uncomfortable with the concept of the world with which we are so familiar continuing perfectly well without us after we have died. How much better it is to hope or believe that there is indeed an afterlife? Such a possibility is, however, viewed by most of us with a mixture of fascination, anticipation and trepidation, if not downright fear.

Many of the world's religions are preoccupied with the question of the continued existence of our souls after physical death. Indeed, some religions teach that this life is merely a preparation for the next and that we will all be judged by the Almighty when we die. Such religions have created elaborate codes of 'do's and don'ts' which we literally ignore at our peril if we wish to ensure a favourable appraisal at the time of our death.

Most religions have created destinations for the souls of the departed. In the case of Christianity, these are Heaven, the place for the righteous and good who can expect a permanent idyllic existence there, and Hell, a state of continuous unpleasant experiences for those who have given themselves over to a life of sin. Some Christians believe in a third destination, known as Purgatory. This is a place where souls have to undertake a process of being tried and tested until a decision can be reached on whether they should be elevated to Heaven or consigned to Hell.

If it is believed that human souls live on after the death of our material parts, it is only a small step to visualize the dead returning to the world of the living under certain circumstances. In many cultures it is thought that the dead yearn to return to the scene of their earthly lives and that they bitterly resent and envy those who they knew and who are still alive. The soul therefore comes back, often angry and seeking revenge, perhaps on someone who it believes wronged it while the deceased was alive. If the life was ended by murder, perhaps it wants to settle the hash of the murderer. There may be all sorts of other reasons why it wants to make its feelings known to the still-living.

On occasions the soul is apparently a trifle confused, but appears to want to sort things out that were left unresolved or otherwise unsatisfactory when its owner died. Perhaps it objects to the manner and place of its burial. Equally, the soul may return if its bodily remains are disturbed or treated with a lack of respect. It may return to provide a warning to someone living concerning their behaviour or perhaps to warn of an impending disaster. A prime time for a ghostly reappearance in the land of the living is on the anniversary of the owner's death. Sometimes perhaps, again if any of this is to be believed, the soul returns simply out of curiosity. Some seem intent on returning and continuing the habitual actions they undertook when they were still alive. Yet others act as if they want to seek atonement for the sins they committed. When it returns, the soul is said to be a ghost. As such, ghosts have both fascinated and frightened humans since the dawn of mankind.

There are many ways in which ghostly phenomena manifest themselves. They may be seen or heard. Often, though, people claiming to have had such experiences say that they have 'sensed' the activity or presence rather than having a more tangible, easily described contact. Perhaps they have smelt the stench of bodily corruption or experienced a sudden and literally chilling fall in the temperature around them. Unexplained footfalls, items rearranged without apparent agency, disembodied sighs and groans, things that go bump in the night. Some claim to have caught images of paranormal entities on film, but the authenticity of such images is disputed.

All these, and a host of other unexplained phenomena, feature in the continuous flow of reports made by people who claim to have had, or think they may have had, encounters with ghosts or other paranormal phenomena. Many of these people are not naturally suggestible, are not attention-seekers and may even be positively stolid and unimaginative. Some were frankly sceptical about the supernatural before they had the experience. It is worth remembering that in most circles, a person talking about the ghostly experiences he or she has had is likely to incur ridicule. Being the butt of mockery makes most people feel uncomfortable. For this reason, it is likely that many unexplained phenomena go unreported and therefore unpublicised.

Some of the stories are what might be called serial hauntings, with what is apparently the same ghost being seen, heard or sensed in and around the same location by many people over a long period. Lincoln and the surrounding district has a fair number of these. Other ghosts have made single or, at best, fleeting appearances – perhaps they completed the purpose for which they came back and, having no further business in this world, returned from whence they came. No one has ever been able to give a satisfactory explanation of one phenomenon – why it seems that ghosts can make their presence known to some people but not others in the same place at the same time.

The 'ghosts' may not even be the returning souls of humans. Ghostly phenomena associated with cats, dogs and horses, for example, also feature in such reports. This raises the fascinating conundrum of whether animals, like humans, have souls which outlive their physical deaths. Some religions, of course, would regard such a claim as quite preposterous. However, if we accept ghostly animals as well as humans, it is worth making the point that they generally seem to be animals with which humans have much contact and with which they can build close, and often fond, relationships. Cats, dogs and even ducks are examples. Someone can put me right, but I have yet to come across a ghost story in this country involving a rat, an adder or a cockroach, for example; these being creatures towards which there is a general aversion. Where does that old chestnut, the coach driven by a headless coachman and drawn by headless horses, fit into the scheme of things?

Children's fictional stories may have ghosts covered in white sheets, rattling chains and emitting screeching noises. In adult fiction, the ghosts are generally more subtle or understated. In the works of that doyen of ghost story writers, M.R. James, the ghosts are little more than hints or suggestions. In spite of being so understated, they are capable of being extraordinarily menacing and malevolent. Truly the icy finger tracing down the spine.

Belief in ghosts is almost as old as the human race. Ghostly phenomena continue to exert a perennial interest, even in the modern world dominated by the rationalities associated with scientific and technological methods and applications. The modern, secular world is deeply imbued with scepticism, which is fair enough, and cynicism, which is less so. Even today in the twenty-first century, a house reputed to be haunted may be difficult to sell or, paradoxically, unusually easy. Each year priests carry out innumerable exorcisms, in all seriousness, intended to bring peace to the living and repose to the spirits of the dead.

Something primeval, some vestigial sixth sense, can cause the tiny hairs to rise on the back of the neck at certain times and in certain places. Frissons of unease, growing into fear and even terror, may cause a rash of goose pimples for reasons we simply cannot explain. We do not like being spooked in real life. However, we love mysteries and most of us enjoy being comfortably scared. Ghosts are big business. Fictional ghost stories, ghost walks, films and documentaries about the supernatural have never been more popular. Spiritualism and psychical research are going strong and still trying to obtain the incontrovertible evidence that will sink the sceptics once and for all. Ghosts remain as much a part of popular culture as they were in the Middle Ages.

Do ghosts exist? If so, what are they? Do they have any objective existence or are they simply the product of superstitious minds, personal suggestibility or overheated imagination? If we accept the claims of serious people that they have had experiences of a supernatural kind, what was it that they actually saw, heard or otherwise sensed? Isn't there a common sense or perfectly mundane explanation for most or all of these phenomena? Even if we do not wish to probe too deeply into these questions, most of can still appreciate a spooky story or movie, can keenly anticipate the thrill of jumping out of our skins at the appropriate moment on a ghost walk or simply take pleasure in finding out about the phantoms, spectres and unexplained phenomena of the place where we live. They are part of the rich and fascinating tapestry of fact, folklore, myth and legend that is local history. There are even serious academic studies made of the subject such as the very readable *The Haunted: A Social History of Ghosts,* by Owen Davies, published in 2007.

One theory of haunting is that ghostly phenomena are a kind of spiritual film, a force generated in places where deeds of violence or great emotional upheavals have taken place. An energy is released which replicates at least some of the sights and sounds of these powerful events. This energy is then infused into the fabric of the places concerned and allows the re-enactment of these events to be experienced from time to time by the still-living, or at least those people apparently receptive to paranormal or psychic phenomena. If there is any substance to this theory, it does account for the disappearance of some habitual or long-established ghosts. The highly-charged emotional ether simply dissipates over time.

If you ask people what kinds of places they expect to be haunted, their responses would probably include 'Gothic' semi-derelict mansions of the sort occupied by the Munsters; the crypts or bone-holes of ancient churches; churchyards; hoary, ivy-clad old ruins; dark and dingy castles; crossroads, where the mortal remains of executed highwaymen used to hang in chains, suspended from gibbets, and also the local lover's leap, the scene over the years of tragic suicides provoked by the miseries of unrequited love. To some extent, such scenarios are clichés. This spiritual film idea, if it has any plausibility, helps to explain why the locations where ghostly activity is reported are often essentially everyday and mundane.

The Lincoln district has more than its fair share of ancient buildings and numerous locations boasting consistent reports of spooky happenings. By no means do all of them fit into the mould of the cliché. Some of the places and sites to be reviewed are remarkable only for their ordinariness, even if the happenings associated with them are anything but ordinary. They include pubs, shops, offices and seemingly ordinary stretches of road. The people who have experienced the ghostly phenomena are the people we would never even glance at should we pass them in the street going about their everyday business. Most are too concerned with the pressures of living in the twenty-first century to go around actively looking for paranormal experiences. Across the country as a whole, it is likely that over a third of the population will admit, perhaps a little shamefacedly, to believing in ghosts. As much as 15 per cent of the population claim to have had experiences which they thought were something to do with ghosts.

The lack of scientifically assembled, rigorously documented and unassailable evidence concerning ghosts only acts to titillate our interest and imagination. A ghost in captivity, readily available for all to see, would surely rob not only the poor ghost concerned but all ghosts of much of that which is so enticing about them: their mystery and elusiveness.

I am a social and cultural historian. This means that I am interested in all types of popular culture and that I want to record, analyse and attempt to explain their significance. Interest in alleged ghostly activity is as old as humanity itself and very much the kind of thing with which a social historian should interact. It is not necessary as a historian that I should believe in, or indeed disbelieve in, ghosts. I do think that some honestly presented reports of strange phenomena have unknown but entirely mundane explanations. People subjected to experiences involving extreme emotions such as terror may not be entirely reliable witnesses. Some reports are made by people seeking attention and publicity – a few days of capricious celebrity. Other reports are by deliberate hoaxers or those with overactive imaginations. It is even possible that some reports have been made by those so bored by their employment that they have tried to enliven their working hours by inventing stories of paranormal happenings. I have worked in jobs so mind-numbingly boring that anything that would help to relieve the tedium was more than welcome.

I have no axe to grind. In what follows, I describe and sometimes attempt to comment on or amplify information that has some my way. In a few cases, readers may discern that I think that someone has been pulling a fast one. A historian's skills require a careful and critical examination and evaluation of information and evidence and this is true when dealing with reports of paranormal activity. I believe that social history should be informative, stimulating and, wherever possible, dare I say it, fun. A historian needs a sense of humour.

For those who make a serious study of psychic phenomena, I am aware that in this book I make technically imprecise use of words like apparition, phantom, wraith, revenant, poltergeist, spectre and spirit. I can only apologise to the experts for this, while believing that the terminology used here is adequate for the general reader. However, a little clarification may be in order and a brief glossary is included.

The names of pubs, shops and other businesses can change overnight or, of course, disappear altogether. As far as I am aware, the names used here were correct as of February 2009.

Three

THE CITY OF LINCOLN

Battles of Lincoln

Lincoln was the scene of two battles, the first in 1141 and the second in 1217. That in 1141 occurred in the vicinity of the West Common. This was the most important armed confrontation in the civil war of 1139-53 between King Stephen and the rebels contesting the throne who supported Matilda. It was by no means a major battle and it is likely that fewer than 100 fatalities occurred. The rebels won, managing to capture the inept Stephen and carry him off to be ransomed – always regarded as a handy way of raising cash in those days. The second was more a brouhaha than a battle. This occurred when a rebel force, mostly of French origin, was attempting to overthrow King John. In this case the fighting took place close to the castle gates and around the street now called Steep Hill. Medieval battles were enormously confusing operations and it is quite clear that in this case the opposing sides never really managed to get to grips with each other. Only two were killed on the King's side and three on the rebels', but a great deal of noise was created. So minor was this skirmish in the scheme of things that it has rather derisively earned the nickname 'Lincoln Fair' or the 'Tournament of Lincoln'.

It is common for reports to be made by people claiming to have seen ghostly visual re-enactments or heard the sounds of battle. A number of times over the last couple of centuries, people walking in the West Common area have apparently heard a confused cacophony which they likened to the sound of an old-fashioned battle. Those who have done so did not necessarily know that a battle had ever taken place in the neighbourhood. Rather less plausible have been very occasional stories of similar noises coming from the area close to the castle gates.

The Bishop's Palace. This building and others nearby in the Close have been the subject of sporadic reports of ghostly activity.

Black Horse, Eastgate

On the west side of Eastgate, high up on a stone wall, is a grotesque carving of a human head. It looks towards the former pub on the other side of the street. Local legend holds that it was placed there by a Bishop of Lincoln in either the sixteenth or seventeenth century, as a silent sermon in stone admonishing those members of the clerical community serving the cathedral who whiled away much of their time in boisterous drunkenness in this pub which was so close to the precincts. It was clear that they could not avoid the temptation presented by having bibulous pleasures on their doorstep, as it were.

The pub has ancient origins and the ghosts to go with its age and history. One of them is that supernatural habitué of pubs across the land, a 'Grey Lady'. She apparently levitates effortlessly in the upstairs parts of the building, dressed in the clothes of an affluent woman of the Victorian period. Recognition is rendered difficult because those who have seen her, and there have been many of them over the centuries, say that her face is blurred. Occasionally she has been glimpsed going for a walk in the vicinity of the former Black Horse.

During the 1990s, the pub underwent a very complete renovation and refurbishment. Such work often seems to produce a supernatural reaction as if whatever spirit is present, perhaps quiescent for years in the building, is then suddenly thrust out of its comfort zone by the bangs, crashes, sounds of machines and human shouts associated with the project. It seems that this intrusion can be resented and the spirit will show its annoyance in the various ways open to it. In the case of the Black Horse, the psychic energy manifested was largely of the poltergeist sort. These included disembodied footsteps, the irritating movement

Left and below: *Ancient carved head, Eastgate.*

of objects around at random, the disappearance of other items, the rattling of door handles and two occasions when objects, fortunately not too hard or heavy, were seemingly thrown at people working in the pub. All this was pretty routine poltergeist stuff, but the most unusual occurrence took place during the rewiring of the building. The mains electricity was switched off and temporary, rather dim, lights powered by a generator were in use. Several men were busily at work when suddenly the whole building was suffused in bright light as all the lights came on. No one has ever been able to provide an explanation.

Strange phenomena continued after the refurbishment had taken place and the building was still trading as a pub. Objects continued to be thrown about and the sound of voices, including those of children, could be heard with no sign of who was making the noise. Stranger still was the occasion when, with the pub having closed its doors for the night, two of the staff decided to have a private drink to relax after a busy evening session. It was a cold night and they decided to put a few logs on the fire. No sooner had they done so than the fire flared up as if paraffin or another highly combustible substance had been placed on it. If that wasn't scary enough, a most baleful, eldritch howling started up in the chimney. Both said that it was as if whatever was doing the howling emerged from the chimney and invisibly swirled around the room. It was accompanied by a marked drop in the temperature. Fortunately the fire soon subsided, but what had been intended as a cosy fireside chat was the last time the two of them decided to stay on after-hours.

Blacksmith's Arms, Bracebridge Heath

Bracebridge Heath stands on the high ground close to the city in the south-easterly direction. The pub has a friendly resident ghost known to all as 'Gordon', who is given to that popular pastime of watching while others work. He usually does so with a benevolent smile. He has been described as having curly black hair and wearing a long grey coat. It is clear that sometimes he becomes irritable and decides to break something – fortunately he always seems to choose an item that isn't worth much. If he is then sternly told off, he clearly takes it to heart because he doesn't do anything else naughty for a while.

Brown's Restaurant and Pie Shop, Steep Hill

Located in the fashionable, tourist part of Lincoln up the hill, this restaurant occupies an attractive and venerable timber-framed building precisely of the sort which looks as if might contain a ghost. That is to say it does not looks in any way scary, just atmospheric. Any student of hauntings will tell you that a seemingly disproportionate number of pubs, cafés and other eating places have provided reports of spooky activity. So it is with Brown's Pie Shop, which has something of the feel of an eighteenth-century city chop house.

The resident ghost has become so familiar that he goes by the affectionate name of 'Humphrey'. Most of the time he manifests himself to members of staff working in the kitchen simply by making them feel that they are being watched. This is disconcerting at first, but the kind of thing that most people can get used to. However, Humphrey has a mischievous side to him and it is possible that he is actually a poltergeist, although such phenomena do not usually stay around over periods of months or even years. One head chef, often the first on the premises in the morning, learned that it made good sense before he got down to work to call out a greeting to Humphrey. Failure to do so seemed to make the unseen Humphrey take umbrage. His petulance has taken the form of throwing things about, causing confusion by moving objects around, turning lights on and off and even mixing ingredients meant for very different dishes. On one occasion, this particular head chef was unable to make it into work and someone else had the job of getting the place going in the morning. He did not know about the requirement to salute the invisible Humphrey. He was preparing vegetables when he was called away to the phone. When he returned to the kitchen, he found the knife he had been using embedded blade-first in the floor, still moving slightly and clearly having just been thrown with very considerable force.

Is there any connection between Humphrey's activities and the uncomfortably cold sensations that are sometimes experienced in a room at the top of the building, which members of staff find so disconcerting that they avoid going there if at all possible? Is Humphrey in any way responsible for other unexplained and rather sinister events, which have included a

bunch of keys being hurled out of a keyhole and then dropped onto the floor by an unseen hand, and footsteps in upper rooms when those below knew no one living could possibly be upstairs?

Overall, Humphrey and his possible unknown companions are more disconcerting than frightening but his, or their, presence is not all bad. One or two witnesses say they have seen Humphrey and that he is a small boy aged about eight! He has become something of a minor celebrity and it is possible that among those who go to Brown's for the excellent food, there are some gourmands who also go in the hope that

The interior of Brown's Pie Shop, Steep Hill.

they may have a paranormal experience. Ghosts, poltergeists and other spirits are, however, notorious for being uncooperative. It is unlikely that they will leave disappointed with the food or the service, but evidence of the supernatural may not come their way. At least one customer, however, did admit to being a little put out during her meal because she had been fixedly stared at by the figure of a small child for much of the time.

In a room which has a dormer window overlooking Steep Hill, the sound of coins being thrown around can be heard from time to time.

Bunker's Hill

Bunker's Hill is the extension of Wragby Road to the eastern fringe of Lincoln. It is also the name of a residential district. A well-known landmark is a spinney with the strange name, 'the Hedgehog'. The fields in its vicinity and 'the Hedgehog' itself have the reputation of being haunted. Many people out walking their pets, riding ponies and children playing have all reported the uncomfortable feeling of being watched and have occasionally glimpsed dark humanoid figures which, thankfully, keep their distance. One woman out with her dog in the dark reported that the animal suddenly shot off, leaving her with the uncomfortable sensation that a man was following her, dogging her footsteps and getting ever closer. With considerable courage she turned round and flashed her torch to reveal what she described as a figure dressed like a monk who looked 'long-dead'. Fortunately, her pursuer clearly didn't like the light and he instantly vanished into the darkness. Is this the same spook who follows people while managing to produce the unmistakeable sound of footsteps, especially on freshly-fallen crunchy snow? Whatever it is can also produce footprints.

Explanations for these phenomena range from the ghost of someone murdered there 100 or more years ago to the spirits of Romans who had a settlement in the vicinity. Archaeologists have found abundant evidence of their past activities, particularly in the form of pottery fragments.

Old Bakery Bistro and Wine Bar, Burton Road

This was housed in a former bakery which closed in 1954, not because the business failed, but on account of the owner's wife having died and the widower simply being unable to cope with life without her. He disappeared without trace.

It seems that his ghost may have returned to haunt the premises. A subsequent owner first became aware of strange happenings when renovation work started on what had become a semi-derelict building. As mentioned elsewhere, ghost activity often seems to be stimulated by such work. Lights switched on and off for no apparent reason and doors opened and closed even if they had been securely bolted. The ghost seems to have been reticent and only allowed himself to be seen on rare occasions, when he was described as being an old man with white hair wearing a long, black robe. Was it his presence which was responsible for sudden drops in the temperature?

The owner herself wasn't troubled by his presence but he obviously did something that one particular overnight guest couldn't stomach. He left after just one night muttering darkly about being woken up by an unpleasant presence in his room and being so scared that he hadn't even dared to put the light on. He'd booked in for a week!

Castle Hill

In the many places across Britain where judicial executions were carried out, there are stories of felons condemned to death, receiving a reprieve and pardon at the very last minute, possibly just as the

The Old Bakery Bistro, Burton Road.

hangman had them in his greedy clutches. Other stories tell of official reprieves arriving just as the poor wretches had been despatched to meet their maker, and while they were still convulsively kicking out in their death agonies. Such stories often contain an explanation or what is really an excuse, either way admittedly of cold comfort for the deceased. It might be, for example, that the horse of the messenger bearing news of the reprieve shed a shoe, the replacing of which, while carried out as quickly as possible, took what proved to be a fatal twenty minutes. Fatal, that is, for the condemned prisoner. In some of these tales, the ghost of the executed felon returns to haunt the scene of the execution or perhaps the cell in which he whiled away his last miserable days and nights. On occasions the ghost is said to have been observed at the place where he supposedly committed his heinous misdemeanour. It is difficult to say how much credence should be given to such tales of tragically missed last-minute opportunities for the reprieve of a condemned felon.

The Castle Hill area of Lincoln has one such story, albeit with variations. It seems that there was indeed an occasion on which a prisoner was awaiting imminent execution in the castle when the decision was taken elsewhere that the sentence would be commuted. A messenger was despatched to ride pell-mell to Lincoln to inform the authorities of the reprieve. One version of the story states that he was riding at full tilt when the horse stumbled and threw him. He broke his neck when he hit the ground, dying instantly.

Castle Hill, looking towards Exchequergate.

Another version maintains that the messenger stopped off for liquid refreshment at a wayside inn but finding the ale good and the company congenial, he forgot the urgent nature of his mission, got drunk and then incapable and was put to bed to sleep it off. In the morning, as the full extent of his negligence filtered through to his still-befuddled senses, he realised that not only had a man died needlessly because of him, but that his own superiors would be requiring an explanation of his actions, or, more specifically, his inactions. No acceptable excuse could possibly be put forward and so, unable to face the music and perhaps overcome with remorse, he saddled up, mounted his steed and galloped off into the great blue yonder, never to be seen again.

All this may, or may not, have had a bearing on the reported experience in 1992 of a man who had been on the night shift and was making his way home up Steep Hill at a time when most folk were glad still to be in bed. No one else was about, the air was fresh and invigorating and the man, although tired, was used to the climb and was feeling pleasantly at one with the world, looking forward to a cup of tea and then his bed. His peace was rudely shattered when a magnificent sweat-flecked black horse ridden by a man in old-fashioned clothes suddenly dashed out of the Cathedral Close through the Exchequergate and hurtled past, only a few feet away. Any closer and he might have fallen under its hooves. The understandably frightened man then described how, as the rider approached the actual gate of the castle, he shouted, almost screamed, to those inside to open the gate. No sooner had the sound died in the air, than both horse and rider simply vanished.

Our friend continued frequently to make his way home after work up Steep Hill and across Castle Hill in the witching hours, but he never witnessed a repetition of this uncanny experience. The author has, however, met two other people who claim to have witnessed something at least partially similar. On both occasions it was in the early morning when few people were up and about. The first was a winter morning, frosty and pitch black yet star-spangled. The second was one of those marvellous dawns in June; bright, cool, fresh, a clear sky and a sense of infinite promise for the day to come. Neither of the witnesses saw anything, but both claim to have heard the sound of a horse galloping over the cobbles on Castle Hill and apparently coming to an abrupt halt, if their ears could be trusted, in the vicinity of the castle gate. The area was otherwise absolutely silent at the time, but the noise made by the horse was quite unmistakeable. Both witnesses were understandably shaken by their experience. Neither of them said that they had ever heard of the incident in 1992.

Castle Hill Club

Several ghosts manifest themselves in the Castle Hill Club. One lurks in the billiards room and, when it has caught the eye of the observer, promptly disappears. Another, which perhaps wisely never allows itself to be seen, is an inveterate bottom-pincher. It is obviously bottoms that turn it on and it is as happy to pinch a male posterior as a female one. It usually inhabits the bar area. As well as having their bottoms pinched, staff, especially after closing time, often have the sense that they are being watched.

The club was formerly the Black Boy Inn and among former guests were the great engineer Isambard Kingdom Brunel (1806-59) and William Marwood (1820-83), the hangman. Brunel was engaged in 1833 on work surveying the Fossdyke Canal and Marwood would have been providing the terminatory services for which he was celebrated, if not by his victims, in the prison close by. It is claimed that the ghosts of both men return on occasions and Marwood's ghost has allegedly been seen looking out of the room where he normally stayed. This is the window in the gable on the east end of the building. Marwood was born at Horncastle and is buried there, so he doesn't have too far to come when returning to the scene of his former activities.

The Castle Hill Club.

The billiard room,
Castle Hill Club.

Centurion, North Hykeham

The Centurion is a modern hostelry, not at all the kind of pub where anyone would expect to see a ghost. But only a few years ago a man having a quiet drink looked up to see, some distance away across the bar, a woman of old-fashioned appearance who looked as if she was just getting ready to go to bed. Surprised, he turned momentarily to his friend to tell him what he had seen. When he looked up again, the figure had vanished. Enquiries of the bar staff made it quite clear that there was no such person on the premises.

Ceres House

If you were to ask people to describe what they think of as a typical haunted building, the odds are on that it would be an old church, an ivy-clad ruined castle with gloomy dungeons or perhaps a mock-Gothic nineteenth-century villa complete with bats, dust-encrusted spiders' webs and pointless turrets and towers. Ceres House simply does not fit any of these stereotypes because it was only built in the late 1970s, in the characterless style so often employed on buildings intended for use by local or national government agencies.

However, Ceres House hit the local headlines some years ago. A man employed on the premises was on his own, having a tea-break, when he spotted an ill-defined patch of mist moving around and apparently disappearing through a wall. At the same time that there was a disconcerting fall in the temperature. He was convinced that at the centre of this moving shape there was a human being. He was understandably shaken by this experience and he reported it to one of the managers who immediately carried out an inspection. The mist did not reappear, but the manager had to agree that there was an eerie and abnormal chilliness in the vicinity. There has been no repetition of this phenomenon, but those interested in the world of the psychic say that the manifestation might relate to some event, perhaps a tragic or highly-charged one, that occurred on the spot many years before Ceres House was built.

Cornhill Vaults

The Cornhill Vaults, now retail premises, was a city-centre pub fashioned out of part of the undercroft of the former Corn Exchange. A comparatively recent manifestation was that of a young man who came up to the bar and then vanished when a member of staff moved to serve him. They were left confused, wondering if they had been seeing things. It seems that this mysterious figure was only visible to a limited number of people. All that the young man left behind was an unpleasant chill in the air. Someone or something had an infuriating habit of tampering with the barrels and pipes in the cellar, a common occurrence in pubs. Could this have been the shadowy old lady wearing dark clothes who was seen from time to time?

County Assembly Rooms, Bailgate

Lincoln has been the commercial and social centre of a sizeable and largely rural region for a long time. It was for the purpose of housing important events in the social calendar that the County Assembly Rooms were opened, probably in 1745. This building has hosted many activities over the succeeding years, by no means all of them polite and pleasant social occasions. Among these were gambling for high stakes, which led inevitably to

accusations of cheating, frayed tempers and worse. It is alleged that disputes led to duels, sometimes with fatal outcomes and even to a few murders on the premises. It is perhaps the latter that has given the building the reputation of being haunted.

The best-known ghost seems to be an anachronism because it has been described

Entrance to the County Assembly Rooms, Bailgate.

The exterior of the County Assembly Rooms, Bailgate.

as a man dressed like a showy cavalier of the seventeenth century. Was he a leftover from something that had had happened on the site before the Assembly Rooms were built, or was he simply someone who liked dressing in a retro style? Members of staff have seen him flitting about from time to time, mostly in the area of the ballroom. For all his exuberant clothes, he seems a coy fellow and he vanishes from sight as soon as he catches the eye of an observer.

The County Assembly Rooms have a number of places which can be unpleasantly cold on occasions. The sound of unaccountable footsteps, the inexplicable opening and closing of doors and the mysterious movement of various items without any apparent human agency have also been reported.

In 2005 a team of paranormal investigators spent a night on the premises (with permission). There were several unexplained, although not particularly spooky, phenomena. The only one which really surprised everyone was the turning on of a very stiff hot water tap by an unseen hand or force.

Drury Lane

Drury Lane is one of the network of ancient streets in the castle and cathedral area of the city. One day in the 1970s, a man who, on his admission, was not of an imaginative or suggestible frame of mind, claimed that he was walking up Drury Lane when a human head came rolling down the hill from the direction of the cathedral.

Drury Lane looking towards Castle Hill.

There have been many apparent sightings of a woebegone woman whose ghost is seen walking in Drury Lane. Is there any connection between this peripatetic apparition and the owner of the rolling head?

Ermine Estate

The Ermine Estate stands on the north side of Lincoln. A few years ago, a family of five who lived on the estate reported that one of them, a young man of twenty-three, had been haunted by the ghost of a woman called Sarah from the moment they took occupation of the house two years earlier.

Things were moved about unwontedly in his bedroom, there were sudden marked falls in the temperature and he, and only he, heard a female voice saying that her name was Sarah. The young man became quite stressed when these phenomena began to occur, but the other family members were decidedly sceptical at first. When it was perfectly obvious that he wasn't swinging the lead, they began to take the matter more seriously. Then they unexpectedly found a photograph and some documents hidden away beneath the floor of the garden shed. These related to a 'Sarah Crow'.

Some research came up with the information that a Sarah Crow had been born at Thorpe-on-the-Hill, close to Lincoln, in 1871. Was this the self-same Sarah who spooked the young man in this house in the twenty-first century?

Good Lane

Good Lane leads off the west side of Newport. An apparently ordinary terraced house was haunted by a ghost who made a habit of moving curtains and invisibly turning electrical appliances on and off. It was thought that this spirit belonged to a woman with the extraordinary name of Fanny Duckmountain. She owned land in the area and died in the 1880s. She was a local character, a pig-owner and apparently much wealthier than her tatterdemalion appearance would suggest.

Green Dragon, Waterside North

The Green Dragon is an ancient timbered building close to the River Witham where it flows, albeit almost invisibly, in the guise of a canal through the city centre of Lincoln. The pub contains the ghost of a little old lady who may be a previous occupant from the nineteenth century, perhaps the proprietor of the building when it was a shop. She has been seen on several occasions, sometimes sitting in the bar smoking a clay pipe and dressed in old-fashioned clothes. Presumably she now smokes outside as all law-abiding punters do, of course. She doesn't seem to be entirely harmless. At least one member of staff threw in her job, being unable to tolerate what she felt was the malign presence of the old woman.

Is she connected with the strange events of the 1990s? One Hallowe'en the new landlord had bolted and barred the doors after closing time when he heard the noise of boisterous merriment coming from the inside of a room that he had locked only minutes before, even though he knew it was empty of people? Perhaps understandably, he

The Green Dragon, Waterside North.

decided not to open the door to see who was roistering inside, but the sounds of jollification ceased abruptly as midnight sounded. After this unexplained event, the pub experienced some fairly typical poltergeist activity. Furniture could be heard being moved about by invisible hands, beer taps were turned on and off, seemingly at times intended to cause the maximum nuisance, and bottles were smashed. No such activity has been reported in recent years.

Greestone Stairs

The Green Dragon pub sign.

Climbing on foot from the city centre of Lincoln to the area around the castle and cathedral is not a mission for the faint-hearted. There are a number of options to get from 'Downhill' to 'Uphill' but with little to choose between them as to the physical effort they require. It is probably fair to say that Steep Hill is the best-known ascent, the one which the tourists and visitors tend to use. Some free amusement can be had from observing the reddening faces of those doing the climb and their seismic inhalations and exhalations as they approach the summit.

Greestone Stairs, or Greestone Steps, which take the walker to the eastern end of the cathedral are a less-used route but are similarly demanding. They are haunted by the ghost of an aged clerical gentleman who has been seen on a number of occasions, apparently appearing and disappearing at will. He has the very handy ability, albeit one disconcerting to the observer, of seemingly being able to melt away and pass through solid masonry. It is said that this is the ghost of a long-deceased clergyman who committed suicide by hanging, possibly from the arch through which the stairs pass.

Greestone Place seems to share the haunted habit with the nearby steps. During the Second World War, the residents of one of the houses were suddenly awoken in the small hours by loud banging noises. These were so frightening that they dashed downstairs, through the front door and outside into the street. Having recovered their equilibrium some while later, they re-entered the house, but the most careful of searches revealed nothing untoward, nothing that could have made the noises.

About twenty years ago, a young woman was climbing the steps when the temperature suddenly dropped, although she herself was warm from her exertions. A sudden silence descended and she saw what she described as the figure of a woman in old-fashioned diaphanous clothes, somewhat like a nun, and cradling what appeared to be a baby in her arms.

Looking down Greestone Stairs.

Looking up Greestone Stairs.

Drunken lamppost, Greestone Stairs.

A diabolical face over a gate, Greestone Stairs.

She seemed to be floating a few inches above the ground and she moved quickly, as if by some invisible form of propulsion. She moved away and vanished from sight.

One evening in 2006, at around 9.30 p.m., two sisters interested in ghosts were taking photographs with digital cameras on the Greestone Steps. When the images were put on computer, one of them showed what looked like a faint image of a ghostly galloping horse.

Not to be outdone by the head that allegedly rolls down Drury Lane, Greestone Steps had a rolling head of its own which, given the incline, probably rolls somewhat faster. Some say that it is the head of a former bishop, removed from a reliquary in the cathedral. An old stone building, in fact once used as a tithe barn, is now used for educational purposes, but apparently it acts as the base for the ghost of a female apothecary who sometimes comes out onto the steps and invisibly touches passers-by and exudes a very powerful aroma of lavender.

Guildhall, High Street

This building and the archway known as the Stonebow alongside were originally built in the fifteenth century. The Guildhall is reputedly haunted by the ghost of a murdered monk.

The Homestead, Bracebridge Heath

Bracebridge Heath is just south of Lincoln on the ridge of high ground running south towards and beyond Sleaford. Although this ridge is not very high, around 200ft above sea

The Guildhall.

level, it does overlook much of the western suburban development of Lincoln which is on the flat lands around the River Witham.

The Homestead is an impressive Victorian house currently in use as a restaurant and pub. In 2004 a perfectly ordinary family party was enjoying a meal when one of them, a boy of four, became distressed by a nasty-looking man who he said was staring at him and making him feel frightened. Indignantly, a couple of men in the party looked round in the direction to which the boy was pointing, intent on giving the man a good talking to. There was no one answering the description, but the boy was insistent that the man was still there and still staring at him. The family was convinced that the boy was indeed seeing something, even if it was only he who could see it. Subsequent enquiries confirmed that other diners had seen or sensed something similar.

The Homestead and its uncanny happenings came under intense public scrutiny for a brief period. It emerged that a 'Grey Lady' (how's that for being original?) occasionally manifests herself in various rooms on the ground floor, while the indistinct figure of an old man is seen lurking in the bar. Was he the reason for the little boy's fright? A young man came forward who related that some years earlier, a husband and wife team who ran the place were forced to move out by repeated scary experiences, including floods in the cellar when barrels were tapped by an unseen hand. Glasses and bottles were moved about and sometimes smashed, and items of all sorts disappeared only to reappear in unpredictable and usually inconvenient places. Worst of all, the sound of something heavy and unyielding (a body?) being moved about upstairs was heard when there wasn't anyone up there to do the moving. When the wife woke up one night to see two figures in her bedroom, the couple decided it was time to quit and leave the spooks to their own devices.

The Homestead pub, Bracebridge Heath.

The Homestead is a surviving part of the former St John's Hospital which closed about twenty years ago. Previously the complex had been known by the brutally unambiguous name of the County Lunatic Asylum. It is known that a former inmate of this forbidding-sounding institution hanged himself at the top of one of the sets of stairs. Could the various strange phenomena that have been experienced in and around the Homestead have anything to do with the troubled lives of some of its former inmates? St John's was an absolutely massive establishment. It has stood empty, gradually becoming derelict, and is scheduled to be the centrepiece for a huge housing scheme in which many of its buildings will be renovated as modern desirable residences. In its present state (February 2009), it is a rather sad remnant of a fine, if somewhat gaunt, set of buildings. It takes little imagination to visualize its cold passages and empty wards witnessing the nocturnal activities of the ghosts of its former residents.

Former County Lunatic asylum, Bracebridge Heath.

Jew's House, Steep Hill

The Jew's House, close to the bottom of Steep Hill, is a remarkable survival. Albeit with some alterations, this is a stone-built twelfth-century townhouse of two storeys which would have been a very superior domicile by the standards of the time. It is also one of the oldest domestic buildings in Europe. It stands in what was part of Lincoln's Jewish Quarter. Close by is Aaron the Jew's House, which dates from around the same time, and a number of other buildings associated with the former local Jewish community. Whether Aaron the Jew ever lived in this particular house is disputed.

The house was once occupied by a Jewish resident who was hanged in 1290 for the crime of coin-clipping. This was the criminal act which consisted of shaving off a small portion from a coin made of a precious metal such as gold or silver. The tiny sliver removed was usually taken from the edge and if this was done systematically and over time, the

The Jew's House.

metal clippings could be accumulated by the offender, melted down and converted into bullion. Coins made of gold or silver, which are relatively soft, become worn in constant use. For this reason they actually become lighter and less valuable. Since people were used to older coins becoming worn in this way, those that had been deliberately clipped were not necessarily easy to detect. The law took a very dim view of clipping because if it was done on a considerable scale, and it often was, it undermined the currency and therefore the stability of the economy. Those found guilty were liable to be executed and that is the fate said to have befallen a former resident of the house, who went to his death in 1290.

Over the years there have been many reports of unexplained activities in the Jew's House. It seems to be the upper parts of the house that are haunted, because those below often hear footsteps going up stairs and then treading rather heavily as they pass to and fro, sometimes apparently for hours on end. Doors creak open or closed on poorly-oiled hinges in parts of the building where there aren't any doors and there are occasional strange bumping noises.

Jolly Brewer, Broadgate

Why is it that so many pubs seem to have ghosts? It sounds cynical, but it is evident that having a reputation for being haunted does a hostelry no harm; rather the opposite. That consideration aside though, the pub, the tavern, the inn or the hotel provide an almost unrivalled setting for human drama. They have witnessed turbulent priests, highway robbers, smugglers, fugitives from the law, all kinds of fools and knaves and every type of human foolishness and frailty. Crimes have been planned in them and the proceeds of crime shared out, illegal transactions of all sorts have been executed within their walls and they have been the trysting places for lovers enjoying or enduring covert relationships. What outbursts of emotion such places have hosted!

The connection between hostelries and ghosts was put very aptly by James Wentworth Day, the well-known writer on ghostly affairs, in his introduction to *The Haunted Inns of England* by Jack Hallam, published in 1972. This is some of what he said:

> No house should be more haunted than an ancient inn. The inn is almost the microcosm of humanity. To it come the traveller on his way, the lonely in search of company, the friendly and the ribald to join in merriment, the gloomy to forget their gloom, the poor in search of warmth, the old to recapture memories, the young to meet their friends and sometimes those tired of life to end their life. Add the highwayman of old, the footpad of past centuries and the thugs and burglars of today…and you have pretty well a complete cross-section of the good and bad in mankind. Rich ground to breed ghosts.

The Jolly Brewer pub sign, Broadgate.

Acknowledging the truth of what Hallam says, it is necessary to make the point that reports of ghostly activity in pubs frequently take very similar, even tediously similar, forms. Sudden drops in temperature, taps on the shoulder or other parts of the anatomy from unseen hands, items moved around with no apparent agency, likewise lights turned on and off, beer taps turned on with no one to do the turning, the feeling of a malevolent presence in the cellar, the mysterious stranger in the bar, the grey figure of a former potman, the wraith disappearing through a wall where once there was an entrance to a tunnel; and so it goes on.

For this reason, it is something of a pleasure to report on the supernatural story attached to the Jolly Brewer. It is certainly refreshingly different, because here an unseen presence calls out the names of staff working on the premises. It is a mystery how whatever does the calling knows these names and also a mystery how and why the spectral voice can be heard over the general din when the pub is busy, but only by those employed there.

There are many pub names starting with the word 'Jolly'. It is perhaps a little bit of 'spin' which gives the impression that the place concerned had a convivial and happy atmosphere. Who, after all, would want to drink in a pub with the name 'the Gloomy Misanthrope'?

Kingsley Street

Kingsley Street is off Burton Road in the 'Uphill' area of Lincoln. It is a pleasant residential street with houses largely of the Victorian period. There have been many reports of noises made by what has been described as a phantom bugle-blower.

In the early 1960s, one of the houses in the street gained temporary fame for being haunted by a ghost known as 'Alf'. He moved in when a husband, wife and three young children took up residence. He was mischievous, although not malicious. His favourite trick was to take a heavy kitchen door off its hinges and leave it standing up against the wall. He did this noiselessly but when he disturbed bedclothes, the sound of rustling could always be heard. It was Alf who apparently caused the letterbox to open whenever someone knocked on the front door. He was given to hiding things, but had one rather unusual stunt up his sleeve. On days when all the windows were closed, he would apparently flick through the pages of a calendar hanging on the wall. In 1963 the family emigrated to Australia. Apparently Alf went with them.

The Lawn

The Lawn is enjoying a renaissance as a social venue, but its origins are as a pioneering hospital for those suffering from mental illness. Attitudes to mental health were just beginning to be more enlightened when it opened in 1820 and, whenever possible, patients would be housed and treated without the close physical restraints previously thought essential for keeping them under control. The Lawn ceased to function as a hospital in 1985, whereupon it was acquired by the City Council and became a visitor and conference centre. Stories are vague, but ever since the Lawn took on its new role, people working on the premises claim to have caught glimpses of woebegone-looking men and women wandering around aimlessly in gowns and apparently looking for something which isn't evident to the observer. Some have

Frontage of the Lawn, Union Road.

Rear of the Lawn.

even said that they have heard distraught crying and wailing – just the kind of noises that might have been expected from the Lawn's former inmates.

Lincoln Cathedral

Without doubt the awe-inspiring sight of the enormous triple-towered Cathedral Church of St Mary astride its hilltop, overlooking the workaday city below and beckoning across the flat lands to the west, constitutes one of the great visual experiences of Britain and, indeed, Western Europe. Not the least fascinating aspect of the cathedral is the way in which it seemingly changes colour in different conditions of weather and light. When the central tower was crowned by a lofty spire and the two western towers by lesser spires, it must have provided an even more dramatic spectacle. The spire of the central tower came down in a great tempest in 1548 and the others were dismantled in 1807.

The construction of the cathedral commenced in 1075 but this building suffered a severe fire in 1141. Extensive restoration work had taken place only for an earthquake to devastate the cathedral in 1185. Rebuilding commenced in 1192 and continued into the fourteenth century, although not everything was plain sailing because the central tower collapsed in 1237. Considerable damage was inflicted on the fabric during the Civil War. Fortunately, the bulk of this great building has survived through to the twenty-first century and it is now rightly one of the most loved and visited of England's cathedrals. Some say that it is the finest cathedral in Britain.

As might be expected with a building of this age, the communities that have worshipped in it, used it for a wide variety of purposes and managed it as a business over the centuries have seen their share of jealousies, intrigues, controversies and venomous ill will. It would not be unfair to say that the activities associated with running the business of the cathedral have not always been conducted in the spirit of love, understanding and tolerance for one's fellows that we have been led to believe are the hallmark of the true Christian.

The west front of Lincoln Cathedral.

Sadly, over the centuries many people who were experiencing the depths of despair chose to make their way into the upper portions of the cathedral and to leap off in an attempt, frequently successful, to kill themselves. Each of these events was a tragedy which involved the outpouring of massive amounts of emotional energy. Christianity commonly regarded suicide as an appalling sin. Until the 1820s, those deemed to have taken their own lives were denied burial on consecrated ground and were interred close to public highways, often at crossroads and with a stake driven through their bodies. It is possible that the stake and the unconsecrated burial were designed as deterrents for those contemplating suicide. The tradition has certainly developed that the stake was used to ensure that the spirit of the deceased was impaled in such a way that it would be unable to get up and move about, causing understandable confusion and terror in the community.

The fact that people have thrown themselves from the cathedral has, perhaps inevitably, led to stories that the anniversaries of their unfortunate deaths have witnessed re-enactments of those fleeting seconds when they plummeted earthwards, perhaps accompanied by shrieks of terror. There are at least five such reported re-enactments. One, interestingly, claims to involve a man who was a bishop of the cathedral. Unfortunately those who have reported seeing him on his downward flight have failed to reveal whether he was dressed in his episcopal robes and accessories. Therefore, this poses the question as to how they

The central tower, Lincoln Cathedral.

The cloisters, Lincoln Cathedral.

know the figure they have seen was indeed that of a suicidal bishop? The records do not mention any of the cathedral's bishops as ever having taken this drastic step. Others include, as might be predicted, a monk, although this building was never a monastic establishment, and two men and a woman. That these last three unfortunates did indeed use the cathedral as their launching pad into eternity is probably not in dispute. More debatable is what the observers actually saw. A group of spectral monks have allegedly been seen in the cloisters.

The best-known supernatural legend attached to the cathedral is, of course, that relating to the 'Lincoln Imp'. This small, grotesque carving can be identified, not always easily, high up on the north side of the Angel Choir at the extreme east end of the cathedral. The imp is a curious figure, apparently sitting and with his right leg crossed over his left. His face possesses a rather mirthless leer. His hands each have three thick fingers armed with sharp claws. He has the ears and horns of a bull and cloven hooves. He appears to be covered in fur, which accords with medieval beliefs that devils, hobs and similar supernatural beings were hairy. The north side of any ecclesiastical building was associated with hell and with evil, so he is in the right place – a reminder to all that evil is to be found, even in such sanctified surroundings.

A host of stories exist explaining the presence of the imp alongside a company of heavenly angels, actually twenty-eight in number. One tells that the Devil and the Wind were strolling in the neighbourhood of the cathedral when the Devil resolved to enter the building to see what mischief he could cause. Rather peremptorily, he told the Wind to wait for him outside

The famous Lincoln Imp.

The Usher Art Gallery.

the building. It was the Devil's misfortune that just as he entered the Angel Choir, a service began. The outpouring of Christian faith this involved frightened the Devil, who flew up high into the choir to consider what to do. Unluckily for him, one of the angels remonstrated with him and, by touching him, turned him instantly to stone. There he remains. The Wind also remains, perpetually whistling around the great building on the hill.

Another version of the story has the Devil joyfully engaged in breaking the cathedral windows. The angels protested but when he persisted, they told him in no uncertain terms to stop. He taunted them, challenging them to stop him if they could. They did. He must have been in the Angel Choir at the time.

Less well-known is the existence of another imp. The legend attached to this one relates that two imps were flying around the exterior of the cathedral trying to find a way in so that they could do some mischief. They flew around for several hours until one of them found the south door open, whereupon he promptly entered. His associate was perhaps made of less stern stuff because he stayed outside. The first imp fluttered into the Angel Choir where he alighted to get his breath back. The moment he settled down, he was turned to stone. The second imp, eventually worn out from flying around, alighted on a buttress on the south side of the cathedral next to the Bishop's Door. He wanted a rest, but no sooner had he landed than he too was petrified.

The legend is charming and attracts many visitors who flock into the Angel Choir eager to seek out the Lincoln Imp. He does not share their sense of fun and gazes down on them in a stony and disdainful silence. Similar stories of impish activities in sacred buildings can be found elsewhere in Western Europe. Whatever the provenance of the imp, the story was ingeniously exploited by the Lincoln jeweller and watchmaker, James Ward Usher. He

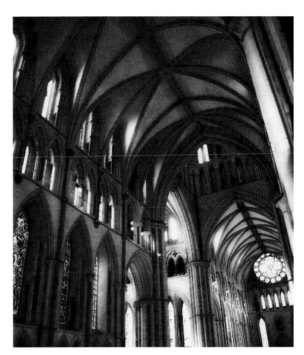

West crossing and transept, Lincoln Cathedral.

was an astute businessman who patented a version of the imp as the design for brooches, cufflinks and other souvenirs, with the implication that these items would bring luck. The imp certainly brought Usher luck a-plenty. He became an extremely wealthy man and when he died in 1921 he left money to build an art gallery and donated his extensive collection of fine art to the citizens of Lincoln. It is of course the Usher Art Gallery, situated down the hill but close to the cathedral, and well worth visiting.

The Bishop's Eye is an exceptionally fine rose window in the main south transept. There is a story that most of the work on the window was carried out by an apprentice, the master being engaged on a task elsewhere. When the window was finished, the master came to inspect it. He was extremely put out to find that not only had the apprentice completed the job satisfactorily, but he realised that the young man had actually done the job far better than he himself could have done. So upset was the master that he decided to commit suicide, which he did by jumping from the triforium close to the rose window. Some people claim they can still discern the stains made by his blood at the spot at which he landed. Inevitably, it is said that his ghost re-enacts the suicidal leap every year on its anniversary.

Lion & Snake, Bailgate

The Lion & Snake is an ancient, partly timber-framed pub reputed to be the oldest in the city. It has been continuously licensed for something like 600 years – a remarkable record. It seems to have more than its fair share of ghosts. Given its position at the heart of the old Roman colony, it is perhaps inevitable that the ghost of a Roman soldier is said to haunt

The Lion & Snake pub,
Bailgate.

the pub's cellar, although what would be achieved by doing so it is hard to say. He is shy and reports of his presence are infrequent. Noises, said to be like that of chariots and of marching soldiers, have also been heard.

Far better-known is the ghost sometimes referred to as 'the granny with the bun'; in this case 'the bun' being the way of arranging hair rather than the edible variety. It is strange that she should be immediately recognizable as a typical granny because while buns on grannies were common in the author's youth, today's glamorous grannies wouldn't be seen dead sporting such an article. Anyway, this old lady has been seen with some regularity for thirty years or more. Her largely unobtrusive presence on the premises has been accepted by successive licensees and their families. When she does decide to obtrude, it is in an entirely unthreatening fashion. She simply walks about upstairs and when any of the pub's living inhabitants squeeze themselves against the wall out of courtesy as she passes, she acts as if they simply weren't there. Her presence has raised the hackles of the pub dog. Who is the old lady?

Not witnessed, or at least not reported recently, is the figure of a dishevelled man who can be vaguely described having a drink in one of the further corners of the bar. Any attempt to have a better look at him or to approach is frustrated by the fact that he gets up and melts into, or rather through, a nearby wall.

A figure, taken to be that of a ghost, has been seen walking nonchalantly through the pub's cellar. It's strange how ghosts seem to have a liking for such places.

Right: *The Lord Tennyson pub, Rasen Lane.*

Below: *The Magna Carta pub close to the Exchequergate. The figure of a ghostly woman has been seen looking out of the room with the bay window. She is supposed to exude the smell of lavender.*

Lord Tennyson, Rasen Lane

A new licensee took over this 'Uphill' pub in 2006 and reported how she and a friend were spooked when they saw a strange apparition half-hidden by a pillar at a time when the pub was closed. Regulars have also seen strange things. One was playing pool when he thought he saw someone he didn't recognise standing at the bar. He looked away for a split-second, in which time the figure must have vanished. A girl working behind the bar saw a man standing in the shadows but as soon as she spoke to him, he simply vanished.

Old Sessions House, Lindum Road

This building at the junction of Lindum Road and Monks Road originated as a gaol for town offenders in 1810. Executions took place there and condemned felons eked out the last miserable days of their often wretched lives in its cold and cheerless cells. When the confinement of prisoners ceased, the building was used as a police station and also as the City Magistrates Court. One night in the 1970s, when it was still in use as a court, a watchman on the night shift was dozing on and off, not worried in the least by his lonely vigil in an otherwise empty building. Unexpectedly, he heard footsteps. Clearly a man of placid temperament, he left his post to investigate, being curious about the noise rather than being frightened of it. The sounds came from the part of the building which formerly housed the condemned cells, but a thorough and careful look through this area failed to establish what had caused the footsteps. The man returned to the cosiness of his little room and was soon dozing fitfully once more. Was the noise caused by the ghost of one of yesteryear's convicted felons revisiting the scene of his emotion-laden last walk from the condemned cell to the scaffold?

Shakespeare Street

Shakespeare Street can be found almost at the furthest, southern end of the High Street. In the 1900s, a house in this street was the scene of an extremely strange occurrence. Whether there was anything of the paranormal about it, assuming the details related are correct, is something for the reader to make his or her mind up about.

A woman living in one of the houses used to tie her son to the bedstead every time she went out to do the shopping. The little lad was only four years of age at the time and quite what he felt about this arrangement has not been recorded. One day, his mother went off on her shopping errand and, as usual, left her offspring under restraint, helpless in the event of a fire or other emergency. When she returned, and she was never gone for long, she was amazed to find the child still in the bedroom, but free of his shackles.

She asked him how he had managed to get loose but all he did was smile, so she picked him up to take him downstairs for something to eat and drink. As she was descending the stairs, she had the unnerving experience of seemingly being attacked by what she could only describe as a large, powerful, but invisible, bird. She claimed that it belaboured her with its wings and pecked her head, producing nasty injuries.

This must have been a chastening experience which she took as a warning because she never left the child alone in the house again!

Smith-Clayton Forge

Ironworks, forges and foundries are not the places that come to mind immediately when tales of ghosts are recounted. As mentioned previously, Lincoln was an important industrial city and the Smith-Clayton Forge produced heavy castings for many customers, including other local engineering concerns.

In the 1980s, the company produced a house magazine called the *Forge News*. One edition carried a photograph on the front cover which set tongues wagging among existing and former employees. The photograph showed a rather indistinct figure which had definitely not been there when the original was taken in 1977. Some readers claimed that they recognised the figure as that of a long-term employee who had died several years previously. Two readers claimed that the image was that of a man who had been killed in an accident in the foundry. Nothing definite was ever established.

St Mary Magdalene, Bailgate

This small church was built at the end of the thirteenth century to cater for local people who had previously worshipped in the cathedral. Space was severely restricted and its churchyard is a couple of hundred yards away, close to the east end of the cathedral and near the top of Greestone Stairs. There is little to see apart from a few low headstones, but rumour has it that the site contains a mass burial pit dating from a visitation of plague in the fourteenth century. It is claimed that periodically the spirits of those interred there rise and illicitly enter the cathedral, where they have some kind of choir practice at midnight.

Strugglers Inn, Westgate

This pub, with its unusual name, also has an unusual sign. It depicts a condemned felon having his arms pinioned on the scaffold. Soon he will be struggling in his death agonies as he hangs in mid-air. It remembers the fact that large numbers of miserable wretches breathed their last in the adjacent castle as the full force of the unforgiving law required them to pay for their criminal ways.

The Strugglers shares a ghost with the castle. It is out of the ordinary by being a canine

ghost, spending most of its time hanging around the castle walls but often scratching at the door of the Strugglers, apparently in the hope of getting some food. If it fails to elicit a quick response, it sometimes barks. The story goes that this dog belonged to a Lincolnshire countryman and general layabout called William Clarke, who was hanged in the prison for murdering a gamekeeper. He managed to evade the authorities for some time but went to his death in 1816. The dog, which was his inseparable companion, lived on. The kind-hearted landlord of the Strugglers felt sorry for the dog and gave him a home,

The Strugglers pub, Westgate.

feeding him, letting him warm himself by the fire and generally making a fuss of him. However, the dog, a lurcher, seems to have been inconsolable about the death of his master and, before long, he went into a decline and died. It was now the landlord's turn to feel inconsolable and he decided to have the dog stuffed and displayed behind the bar. As inevitably happens, time passed, memories lapsed or faded away totally and the stuffed hound came to be regarded as a bit of unwanted clutter from the past, a dust-trap. The stuffed dog was placed in a cupboard for some years but in the 1980s its historical and curiosity value was appreciated and it was taken out, dusted down and presented to the museum in the castle.

Theatre Royal

What exactly is it that causes theatres to be the location for so many stories about the supernatural and paranormal activity? Is it something to do with the setting, the willing suspension of disbelief which is required of their audiences and the sense that what happens on the stage is larger than life? The answer to such metaphysical questions may not be easy to determine, but there is little doubt that a live dramatic performance on stage which really engrosses the spectator is likely also to heighten his or her imagination. Art transposes reality so that we are not sure what is shadow and what is substance. The members of the audience put some of the accepted behavioural mechanisms on hold for the duration so as to enter into the action unfolding in front of them. Emotions are released which are usually carefully husbanded in 'ordinary life'. Do these emotions suffuse their surroundings with a kind of highly-charged ether which provides a congenial atmosphere for anything supernatural?

Lincoln's Theatre Royal lives up to expectations in terms of unexplained events. Not all manifestations of paranormal activity are necessarily easy to categorize. An electrician who worked for the theatre company some years ago was in the auditorium one day when he suddenly had cause to drop his tools and flee outside. All he was able to blurt out was that there was a frightful noise, unlike anything he had ever heard before, coming from an area of seating. Whatever it was, and his was not a very good description, it had a bad enough effect to cause him to leave the company shortly afterwards. He emigrated within a few months, although this action, of course, was not necessarily linked to his unpleasant experience. Subsequently, another electrician heard something similar in the auditorium and resigned shortly afterwards, but again without providing any useful description of what had happened.

It is not just 'sparkies' who admit to having had weird and unpleasant sensations in the theatre. On one occasion, a member of an amateur company was in her dressing room getting ready for a performance when she came down the stairs, screaming hysterically. She rushed out of the building, but not before she had calmed down enough to say that she had seen something. She took no further part in the production. They never got to the bottom of that one, since she was never able to say what it was she saw. A new employee was taken on, mostly to work in the box office, and she had only been there a few days when she asked if the place was haunted. She said that there was an area in the dress circle which was especially cold and dank and had what she described as a 'presence'. One of her friends, who claimed psychic powers, visited the theatre shortly afterwards and stated that there was definitely a supernatural presence around the dress circle.

The Theatre Royal.

Certainly there is something untoward in the seating areas within the Theatre Royal. About thirty years ago, during a matinee performance, one of the staff was alerted when he spotted a man, described as plump, moustached and middle-aged, sitting at the back of the circle and apparently puffing away expansively on a cigar. He was some distance from other members of the audience and the smoke he was producing would perhaps not be a nuisance to them, but that was not the point. Smoking was banned in the Theatre Royal at all times, largely because a fire which destroyed the theatre back in the nineteenth century had been blamed on an unknown person smoking carelessly. Who was this thoughtless, or even arrogant, man who ignored the 'No Smoking' signs which were clear for all to see? The member of staff was incensed and made his way hurriedly to tell him in no uncertain terms to put his pipe out. Unfortunately, he momentarily took his eyes off the man and he was totally flabbergasted when he got to where he had been sitting only to find no man there, nor even a smell of cigar smoke! Enquiries of the other nearest patrons failed to elicit anything. They had neither been aware of the man, nor of the smell of cigar smoke. None of the other members of staff had seen the cigar smoker get up and leave and not surprisingly, our man was beginning to doubt the evidence of his senses. Something that could not be gainsaid, however, was that a seat in the row where he thought the man had been sitting was down. This strongly suggested that there had indeed been someone sitting there. Who was the man? Why was he smoking? How did he vanish? Had he ever really been there?

Other unexplained phenomena at the Theatre Royal include the sound of a seat being lowered, even when the auditorium is empty, and a diaphanous figure once seen climbing a ladder backstage which simply faded away when challenged.

There is an ancient belief that butterflies are the souls of the dead. When they appear in theatres, they are regarded as lucky omens and that the current performance will be a success. Butterflies have been seen in the auditorium on a number of occasions, and often during the pantomime season – the time of the year when such creatures would be expected to be in hibernation. The Theatre Royal is by no means the only British theatre with tales of the untimely, but welcome, appearance of butterflies.

White Hart Hotel

The White Hart Hotel is an ancient and historic inn standing in Bailgate, right at the centre of Lincoln's main tourist area. It is probably a building of fourteenth-century origin. It has had its ups and downs, being described by a visitor in 1649 as urgently needing a lot of money to be spent on repairs and improvements. The frontage onto Bailgate dates from 1840.

The White Hart has witnessed much history over the centuries. We know, for example, that Richard II and his wife, Anne of Bohemia, stayed there in 1387. Richard reigned from

The sign of the White Hart Hotel, Bailgate.

1377 to 1399 and died at Pontefract Castle in 1400 having been deposed by his cousin, Henry Bolingbroke, who went on to become Henry IV. Richard took being forced off the throne so personally that he lost the will to live and literally starved himself to death. However, his visit to Lincoln was in happier times, as he was then quite besotted with his wife. When she died a few years later, probably of bubonic plague, he was so crazed with grief that he had Sheen Palace, where she had died, razed to the ground. Being a king, he could do such things.

The White Hart has witnessed an impressive number of paranormal phenomena over the years. One is a frightened-looking serving girl in a mob-cap who is only seen on the first floor. According to legend, the fear that registers on her face is because she has just realised that a man is approaching and viewing her with evident evil intent in his mind. He is said to have been a local rat-catcher who did indeed strangle and murder her in a drunken frenzy after she had rejected his sexual advances. No wonder that she cowers against the wall! Then there is a strange and rather menacing figure which appears in the Orangery, a restaurant based in the former stables. It is frequently accompanied by a physically and psychologically chilling drop in temperature and is generally believed to be a highwayman who covers up his facial features because he had severe disfigurement, on account of someone once having attacked him with a flaming torch. All that can be seen of his face are his eyes. These peep over the top of just the kind of travelling cloak any self-respecting highwayman would wear when out on a sortie. In addition, of course, he has a tricorn hat, thigh-length riding boots, spurs and a couple of pistols stuck nonchalantly through his belt. He smells of leather and horse sweat. He seems harmless enough, except for the disconcerting habit of abruptly appearing and then disappearing with equal speed. It is thought that he returns in order to get even with his torch-wielding assailant. He obviously hasn't had much success yet – but every dog has its day, and so perhaps his patience will be rewarded.

Back in the 1960s, a young man died after shooting himself in one of the guest bedrooms. Patrons staying in the room involved have commented on strange sobbing noises and a generally sad atmosphere in the room. Another reported ghost is that of a man, clearly well-to-do and dressed immaculately in a smoking jacket and cravat. It is said that while he was staying at the White Hart in 1978, a burglar entered his room and removed, among other items, an attractive and quite valuable antique. He was sufficiently put out by the experience that he chooses to revisit the site of his loss and hence he is glimpsed wandering around in a fashion which suggests that he is looking for something. Some say that he was a dealer in high-class antiques. Others claim that he was actually a crook and con man who persuaded an old woman to sell him a jar at a price way below its real value; according to this version, he died in the hotel as the result of the old woman finding out how much the jar was really worth and then putting a curse on him. A different account is that he is a former owner or manager of the hotel who lived on the premises and was robbed of a very fine ornament referred to as a 'ginger jar'. Now he implores anyone he comes across to return his property.

An extraordinary event occurred in the 1960s when kitchen and serving staff were flabbergasted to observe what appeared to be a patch of bright light which spent some time moving around the restaurant. Fortunately, this was before any diners had arrived. It was not the first time such a phenomenon had happened. Some years earlier a couple were enjoying a candlelit meal in the restaurant's elegant surroundings when there was a sudden flash and a ball of light briefly appeared, following which an unseen force decided to spoil their meal by scattering the cutlery and moving the plates around. Stoically, and with typical British reserve, they didn't want to make a scene, but a scene was being made for them and so eventually they called for the head waiter. Perhaps this cowed whatever was causing the problems, because he assured them the phenomena would stop – and they did immediately!

Strange, inexplicable things continue to occur at the White Hart. In the 1980s, a boy who was the son of the hotel's proprietors calmly told his parents that he was often made ready for bed and tucked in by a friendly old nanny who, although she wore old-fashioned clothes, wasn't really there. The boy evinced no fear or self-consciousness when talking about his mysterious companion and his parents put this down to a not-uncommon childish fantasy. Possibly related to the boy's experiences are occasional sightings of an elderly lady in the costume of the early nineteenth century who walks with some purpose down a corridor in the upper reaches of the hotel and promptly disappears through a wall. Another incident was reported by a couple staying in the hotel who complained that they had been kept awake by the sound of children making a lot of noise as they apparently played in the corridor outside the couple's bedroom. Later on, similar noises came from an adjacent bedroom. Management could only apologise but they were unable to explain the source of the noises. There were no children staying in the hotel at the time! The room from which the noises apparently emanated was empty that night.

Many of the hotel's guests know nothing of the White Hart's reputation for being the home of unexplained and possibly supernatural phenomena. Although the building does not have a sinister feel about it, there must be something about the place that causes visitors' imaginations or sensations to go into overdrive. On innumerable occasions, guests have reported hearing sounds described as being like those of marching Roman soldiers tramping past the building, while others have described in some detail both the sight and the sound of horse-drawn carriages on the cobbles at the front of the hotel with the rattling of harnesses. The White Hart is close to the remains of many Roman buildings and it was indeed a coaching inn during the eighteenth and early nineteenth centuries. It may also have been the rendezvous of highwaymen and, of course, all manner of villains, rogues and scallywags have stayed there over the years. Perhaps they left something behind.

Witch & Wardrobe

This pub overlooks the sluggish River Witham and there have been occasional reports of beer pumps being turned on and off when there is no one around, of the sound of tables and chairs scraping the floor as if they are being moved when there is nobody visible to do the shifting and of items being moved about by an unseen hand. Some items have mysteriously disappeared for days or weeks, only to reappear equally mysteriously either in some other part of the building or where they were originally positioned. Sometimes they seem to have disappeared for good.

The pub name, which is unique, refers to the title of one of C.S. Lewis's popular *Chronicles of Narnia* series of novels for children – in this case *The Lion, the Witch and the Wardrobe*, which was published in 1950.

The Witch & Wardrobe pub, Waterside.

The ghostly sign of the Witch & Wardrobe.

Looking towards the cathedral from the bottom of Steep Hill.

Above: *The top of Steep Hill after dark.*

Left: *The Glory Hole, High Street. A spooky spot, but with no ghostly associations.*

Four

LINCOLN CASTLE

A Little History

Lincoln Castle was one of many founded in England by William the Conqueror. This stern, untrusting and ruthlessly efficient man had castles built across the country to act as bases from which his troops could sally forth to impose the Norman regime on his unwilling new subjects. William was also a strong believer in *realpolitik*, in creating an image which would leave the natives in no doubt as to who was in control and fully intended to stay that way. Castles performed this function admirably. Their imposing, forbidding and formidable bastions reared up to browbeat any of those contemplating continued resistance and rebellion. So it was with Lincoln Castle, on which building work commenced in 1068 after William himself had visited the site. Its position made it a natural stronghold and virtually unassailable on its south side. The *Domesday Book* informs us that 166 dwellings were removed to make way for the castle.

The castle found itself at the centre of 'the Anarchy', the struggle between King Stephen and Matilda in the twelfth century. At first it was held by Matilda, who settled in Lincoln when she came to England in 1140, only for the castle to be taken by Stephen's forces. In 1141, Stephen was defeated in battle and imprisoned by his enemies but by 1146, he was once again in possession of the castle. The castle was in the wars again, literally, during the troubled reign of John, undergoing a prolonged but unsuccessful siege by the barons who had taken Lincoln with the aid of the Dauphin of France. So-called nobles supporting John's successor on the throne, Henry III, occupied the castle during another attempted siege in 1217, supported by French forces. Lincoln Castle had a complicated, if rather less violent, history after this time and having once been a royal castle, it passed through the hands of the Earls of Lincoln and Lancaster

Above: *A ghostly hologram in Lincoln Castle Prison.*
Left: *A cell in Lincoln Castle Prison.*

before reverting to the throne in 1399, by which time the fabric was much decayed. It was held for the Royalists during the Civil War in the mid-seventeenth century, but Parliamentary forces had little trouble in capturing it.

Eventually the castle was bought by the County of Lincoln in 1831, by which time it had seen many years of use as a prison. Opening in the early 1790s, it had at first mainly been used to accommodate debtors who lived under a fairly relaxed regime. They were allowed to leave the castle during the day and undergo paid employment, thereby earning the money with which they could discharge their financial liabilities. The conditions in the prison were, however, notorious even by the standards common at the time. In 1840, new additional accommodation was provided to house serious criminal offenders and it was designed to follow the 'Panopticon' system first employed at Millbank Prison in London. This involved solitary confinement and it was by no means uncommon for the inmates to be driven mad by the stress this involved. A reminder of this system is the sinister prison chapel, of which more will be said later. Perhaps it was just as well that the prison closed entirely in 1878.

The Prison Chapel

Given the grim and gory events witnessed within and around its precincts, it is only to be expected that several stories of hauntings have been reported from Lincoln Castle. Not surprisingly, the prison chapel features in some of these. A female figure described as either 'white' or 'grey' has been glimpsed on many occasions flitting through the chapel. She is thought to be the ghost of a former prisoner who died while serving her sentence in the prison and who clearly has some reason for her apparent unwillingness to settle down.

Lincoln Prison Chapel.

The chapel is a strongly atmospheric part of the castle. It was regarded as an integral part of the Panopticon system, mentioned earlier, in which solitary confinement was used to keep the inmates from communicating with each other. It was felt that they needed to be regularly and suitably chastened concerning their past misdemeanours and their criminal status, and they should show repentance and crave forgiveness while also being appropriately thankful to the Almighty for his infinite mercy. For these reasons, worship was a key part of the regime. Each prisoner would be removed from his or her cell, hooded and then chained to a group of other inmates. Observing strict silence, they would then be marched to the chapel. What follows is the description of this chapel which appears in the Lincolnshire volume of *The Buildings of England* by

Nikolaus Pevsner and John Harris, first published in 1964. Pevsner was a great art historian, but a man of somewhat clinical and austere temperament who rarely allowed emotional matters to influence his judgement of things architectural. This is what he says:

> The chapel…is a unique and terrifying space. Tiers of cubicles, head high, ensured that the convicts could see the preacher but not each other. The side walls of each cubicle hinge to form the doorway into the next, so that the system is self-locking; once in place, the row of felons could only be extracted one at a time, and in order. The detailed design is truly brilliant and truly devilish, a fair reflection of the age which devised philosophical theories to whitewash sending six-year-olds down the mines.

The prisoners would have been unable to see anything but the ranting chaplain in his pulpit. In recent years, dummies representing prisoners have been placed in some of the cubicles and if anything, their presence adds to the sinister atmosphere – even more so because some visitors claim to have seen the dummies moving their heads!

To sit in one of these cubicles in the unlit chapel on a gloomy winter's day when there is no one else about is an experience never to be forgotten, and one which easily allows the imagination to go into overdrive. Perhaps this is what happened to those people over the years who claim to have heard the jangling of great bunches of keys on the chains of unseen phantom warders and the clang as cells doors were slammed shut in cold, cheerless and echoing stone passages. Also reputedly heard have been the despairing cries of the inmates as their cell doors closed and they bewailed the fate that required them to be incarcerated entirely on their own for the next fifteen hours or more.

Interior of Cobb Hall, Lincoln Castle.

Cobb Hall

The chapel is by no means the only part of the castle in which supernatural phenomena have apparently been experienced. The tower known as Cobb Hall has been mentioned at least three times as the scene of a bizarre and inexplicable occurrence. Something regarded as a supernatural presence has apparently picked on a small child and attempted with invisible force to push them down the stairs. Thankfully, on each occasion the children's parents were close to hand. While bemused at seeing their offspring seemingly being pushed by an invisible hand, they reacted quickly and prevented them from falling and possibly receiving serious injuries. The last report of this spot of nastiness is dated 2005. What then is the malevolent force that lurks in Cobb Hall? Is it the ghost of one of the felons who was hanged close by? One of those who had this sinister experience actually saw an old woman dressed in black who vanished before he could recover from his understandable terror. Until 1868, public executions took place on the roof of the tower so that all the spectators could get a good view.

The Lucy Tower

The Lucy Tower is a polygonal shell keep standing on one of Lincoln Castle's two mottes, or mounds. It is thought to have been added to the castle sometime in the twelfth century. Lines of simple grey stones mark burials which took place at this spot, and it is not surprising that over the years there have been reports of distressed voices, wailing with misery or imploring mercy. These do not appear to have been accompanied by any visual phenomena.

The Lucy Tower, Lincoln Castle, from a distance.

The Lucy Tower on its Norman motte.

Gates to the Lucy Tower.

Headstone of a hanged convict, the Lucy Tower.

Above: *The Observatory Tower, Lincoln Castle.*
Right: *Staircase in the Observatory Tower.*

The Observatory Tower

The Observatory Tower stands in the south-east corner of the castle precinct. It is placed on a small mound which may have been thrown up as part of the original Norman motte-and-bailey castle. It consists of eleventh and fourteenth-century masonry and is topped by a picturesque, but slightly silly, battlemented and machicolated extension built in the Victorian period by a governor of the prison who fancied himself as an astronomer. The tower can be climbed and there is a superb, if rather vertiginous, view from the top. The staircase inside the tower is narrow and dark and no place for the fanciful. A climb to the top is on the agenda of most family parties who visit the castle, but some of them have reported scary experiences, even at times when there have been many visitors around. The sensations have included sudden sharp and unpleasant drops in temperature, mysterious figures which have manifested themselves on the stairs only to vanish in the blink of an eye, as well as indistinct shadows in parts of the tower or under conditions of light in which shadows would not be expected. Probably the most disconcerting experience has occasionally been had by people climbing to the top of the tower who claim that an invisible force coming downwards has tried with considerable strength to push them out of the way.

Lincoln Castle Grounds

Under the right conditions, Lincoln Castle is a spooky old place and few people would want to spend time alone within its walls, especially at night and in the dark. There is an almost tangible feeling that high emotions and tragedies have been played out in this place. Perhaps they have imbued the surroundings with a kind of nervous energy.

Above: *A general view of the castle grounds.*
Left: *Staircase in the Observatory Tower.*

Some people can be very suggestible in such places, and it should come as no surprise that other paranormal activities have been experienced around the castle precinct. They include the tormented cries of convicted felons being dragged off to be hanged, the subdued murmur of the crowd around the scaffold waiting for the fatal drop and then the responding gasp from the massed onlookers as the victim was left kicking in mid-air, flaying around in his death agonies. As with so many places where large-scale fighting has taken place, the clanging sounds of iron on iron, the discharge of artillery and small arms, the screams of injured and terrified horses and men and the rallying calls of officers have been heard, or so it is said.

A Ghostly Lurcher

Lurchers are intelligent, resourceful dogs whose existence is not recognised by the Kennel Club. Despite this stigma, it is reassuring to know that they most certainly do exist. The likeable rogue Claude Greengrass had a very fine lurcher called Alfred in earlier episodes of the long-running television drama *Heartbeat*. Among Greengrass's many illicit and illegal activities was a spot of poaching. The ghost of a lurcher, thought to belong to a poacher who was executed for his crimes, has been seen from time to time around the west gate of the castle or anointing the many lampposts that illuminate the open area containing lawns and flower beds within the castle walls. For more on this phenomenon see 'Strugglers Inn', p. 49.

Five

GHOSTS AROUND LINCOLN

Anwick

At the entrance to the churchyard at Anwick, a village a little to the north-east of Sleaford on the A153, two large and curious stones can be found, known locally as the 'Drake Stones'. The strange legend relates that a local farmer was ploughing a nearby field when his horses fell into a boggy morass. They not only fell in – they disappeared from sight and as they were sucked down, a drake flew out of the spot where they had vanished. The next day, local people, understandably lamenting the disappearance of the farmer, were dumbfounded to find that marking the exact point where the farmer and his team of horses had disappeared was a very large stone which could only be described as 'drake-shaped'.

In the year 1832, attempts were made to move this stone but they had to be abandoned because every time they tried, the chains being used simply burst asunder. On one of these occasions, all involved were flummoxed when a drake flew out from under the stone. In 1913, renewed efforts were made to shift the stone and they resulted in the big stone breaking into two pieces which were then placed on their present site. Many people claim they have seen two drakes sheltering under the stones. All this sounds rather as if those volunteering this information have been sampling magic mushrooms.

One explanation put forward is that the stone was sacred to the Druids. The author is unsure as to whether this actually sheds any useful light on the matter. What does help an understanding of this legend, however, is that 'drake' in an alternative word for a 'dragon'. A drake of the wild duck variety flying out of a bog is one thing. If you want to believe in dragons, then anything is possible.

On a by-road south-east of the village stands Haverholme Priory. This was founded in 1139 and was one of the few houses belonging to the Gilbertine Order whose

St Edith's Church, Anwick.

The Drakestones at Anwick.

The gaunt ruins of Haverholme Priory.

headquarters were at Sempringham, not very far away. A house in the Gothic style was built on the site in 1780 and rebuilt in the Tudor style in 1835. Parts of this building survive. Close to the house is a path called the 'Ghost Walk'. A guest in the mid-1990s had a troubled night. He reported the constant sound of feet crunching the gravel. These noises disturbed him and kept him awake. Several times he got out of bed and drew back the curtains, determined to see who the midnight perambulator was and to give him a piece of his mind. There was no point in opening the window and bellowing. Although the crunching footsteps continued, he could see no one who could possibly be making the noise.

In the grounds is a bridge close to a clump of trees. This area is said to be haunted by a spectral nun. This seems entirely plausible since the Gilbertines had mixed establishments.

Haverholme seems to be a haunted neighbourhood. Strange noises have often been heard at night and owners taking their dogs for walks have talked about how their pets were clearly spooked by something undetectable by human senses.

Bardney

The village of Bardney is to the south-east of Lincoln. Close by is the site of what was once a very important Benedictine abbey. The story goes that the monks refused to allow the bones of St Oswald, who died in AD 642, to be buried in the precincts. Oswald's head had already been interred at Lindisfarne and various others of his bits and pieces had been commandeered by monasteries elsewhere on account of the miraculous properties that were ascribed to them. None of this really explains why the Bardney fraternity were so opposed to what was left of the poor man being laid to rest among them. Anyway, someone who came to Bardney with the collection of bones purporting to be St Oswald's remains must have taken umbrage when he was rather bluntly told to put take them elsewhere. Understandably, he simply dumped them on the doorstep and took himself off, doubtless muttering uncomplimentary comments about there being nothing as cold as charity, especially monastic charity.

However, no sooner had the abbey's main gate been secured for the night than a great pillar of light shot up to the skies. Suitably chastened by this sign of God's disapproval, the monks of Bardney had a quick think, gathered up the abandoned bones and had them buried within the abbey precincts while making a pious public statement to the effect that never again would they close their doors to anyone or anything. Poor old Oswald's remains were moved yet again in the year AD 909, this time to Gloucester. However, the phrase, 'Do you come from Bardney?' is still used by older villagers as a gentle admonition for anyone who has not shut the door.

The site of the abbey and its scanty remains are open to the public. Inevitably, there are people who have said that while walking around the site on moonlit nights they have seen a pile of bones transform itself into a skeleton and then proceed to perform a *danse macabre*.

The Priory Farm at Orford, Binbrook

Binbrook is some distance from Lincoln but the story is a good one, so I hope that the reader will forgive this excursion into the wilds of the Wolds.

During the latter part of the nineteenth century, the farm was occupied by a well-to-do farmer who collected antiques and had amassed such a huge collection that he began to store the surplus in the cellar of his old farm building. Occasionally, he sent one of his servant-girls down into the cellar to give them the once-over with a feather duster or a necessary polish. On one particular day, he gave out his instructions before he left to do some business elsewhere. He told one of the girls that she was to spend the whole day in the cellar, there being plenty to keep her busy. When he returned, many hours later, he called and was surprised when there was no reply. He became rather irritated, perhaps thinking that the girl had taken herself off somewhere in the absence of her master. Having failed to find any trace of her, and with the other servants saying that they hadn't seen her all day, he eventually decided to investigate the cellar. There he was horrified to find her lying prostrate and unconscious on the floor.

She was examined by the doctor, who pronounced that she was suffering as the result of having had a severe shock. Try as they would, neither boss not doctor could get her to say anything about whatever it was that she had seen or heard. After a short time away from work, the girl returned, but always politely refused to enter the cellar and refrained, even as the weeks turned into months, from giving any hint of the nature of her shocking experience.

Just what was it down in the cellar that had scared her so badly and struck her dumb, at least so far as saying anything about it was concerned?

Although he never got to the bottom of the mystery, the owner of the farm must have had bad vibrations as a result of this strange episode, because some years later he had the cellar bricked up without having the antiques removed first!

There were already stories in circulation about spooky phenomena in the area and when the story of the servant's experience became well-known, inevitably tales of the horrors lurking around Priory Farm grew more exaggerated by the day. The building was pulled down some years ago.

The Red Hall, Bourne

Now the author is only too aware that some readers will say that Bourne, way down in the south of the county, is a long way from the city of Lincoln. He cannot disagree. He pleads a degree of self-indulgence and asks for a little toleration because this pleasant, small town vouchsafed him one of a few uncanny, inexplicable or possibly even ghostly experiences that he has experienced during his largely wasted life.

Bourne was once a railway centre of some importance. Lines radiated from the town to all four cardinal points. The first of these was southwards. The Bourne & Essendine Railway was opened in 1860 and gave the town access to the route of the Great Northern Railway from London to the north, the major trunk route that later became known as the East Coast main line. The Bourne & Essendine was absorbed by the Great Northern in 1864 and it enjoyed a slow and somnolent existence until 1951 when it closed completely. In 1866, the Spalding & Bourne Railway opened and later became part of a company with greater ambitions, as suggested by its name, the Midland & Eastern Railway. In 1872, the Great Northern Railway opened its route to Sleaford, which closed to passengers in 1930. The final opening was that in 1894 of the line to Little Bytham Junction to the west. This and the line eastwards to Spalding became part of the Midland & Great Northern Joint Railway. Its fabled cross-country line from the East Midlands to the East Anglian coast carried several generations of mostly working-class families from their humdrum or even oppressive industrial surroundings, particularly in Derbyshire and Nottinghamshire, for an all-too-brief annual binge and escape at Cromer, Sheringham, Caister-on-Sea or Great Yarmouth.

Many existing buildings were taken over and adapted for railway use in Britain in the nineteenth century and one of the most interesting is the Red Hall at Bourne. Although the origins of the hall are not absolutely certain, it is thought to have been built around the 1590s and almost certainly by a member of the local Fisher dynasty. Later it came into the hands of the Digby family. This had led to the emergence of a myth which has almost taken on the status of received wisdom. This avers that the Red Hall has a connection with the family of Sir Everard Digby, one of the chief conspirators in the Gunpowder Plot of 1605. The myth has shamelessly been expanded by those who say that the Red Hall was one of the meeting places of the conspirators while they were planning their dastardly deed. Just as the newspapers never let the truth get in the way of a good story, it has even been alleged that the Red Hall is haunted by the ghosts of some of the Gunpowder Plotters!

In 1857, the Red Hall was sold to the Bourne & Essendine Railway Company. It was within a few yards of the railway and it became a rather grandiose stationmaster's house and ticket office. It later came under the ownership of the M&GN who decided that it no longer suited requirements and they proposed to demolish it. This suggestion created an absolute furore in the town and the locals, with the assistance of the Society for the Protection of Ancient Buildings, were successful in preventing the demolition going ahead.

Passenger trains ceased at Bourne in February 1959, while freight services ended in 1965. The Red Hall became redundant when passenger trains finished and its condition was allowed to deteriorate to the extent that it once again became a candidate for demolition. Fortunately, in 1962 it was acquired by the Bourne United Charities and with the aid of various grants, an extensive repair and refurbishment was completed. It then became a community resource greatly appreciated by the townsfolk.

The author used to present courses for the Workers' Educational Association in a room in the Red Hall. One particular course was held on ten winter evenings and on those occasions, a key-holder would appear a few minutes before the meetings were due to start in order to open the building up. The author liked to prowl around the grassy area surrounding the hall, even in the dark, and to speculate on how different the locality must have been when there was considerable railway activity so close by. He remembers very clearly his surprise when, one night, he arrived about half-an-hour early and found the door open but no lights on in the building. Deliberately not turning the lights on, he decided to have a look around the rooms upstairs. They were immensely atmospheric, with the moonlight shining through the ancient windows. They were not threatening

The Red Hall, Bourne.

in any way and there was evidently no one about. He made his way downstairs to the room on the ground floor where the meetings took place, still with ten or fifteen minutes to spare. As he did so, he was amazed to hear the clear and unmistakeable sound of creaking floorboards as someone moved around in one of the upstairs rooms. He called out and went up the stairs again, but there was no one there. The key-holder was extremely surprised to find the author inside because the hall had been left locked. Was it a mysterious human intruder or someone from the other side in the Red Hall that winter's evening?

Branston Hall

Branston is a large village on the B1168 just to the south-east of Lincoln. Branston Hall was built in the late nineteenth century and has had several uses. During its time as a hotel, a number of guests have reported the sound of 1920s-style jazz when there has been no one present to make the sound. A noise like that of a weeping woman has been heard on the main stairs.

Visitors to Branston with an eye for the curious should on no account miss 'Mr Lovely's Gates'. A rather odd house called Stonefield has gates decorated with grotesque monkeys, presumably for a purpose, but certainly one lost on the author. They will be found at OS TF 013 676 (OS Landranger 1:50,000 Series).

Burton-by-Lincoln

Burton is little more than a hamlet and stands just outside the northern extremity of Lincoln on the B1398. Legend has it that on 25 April 1634, St Mark's Eve, two men from Burton held a vigil in the porch of the local church to test the commonly-held belief that on that particular night, the spirits of those local people destined to die in the following year could be seen.

The vigil started at eleven o'clock and the men had sat in the porch for nearly an hour. By this time, they were getting tired and bored when, on the stroke of midnight, the moon went behind a cloud and the flickering light of handheld torches could be seen approaching the church. They recognised the vicar, walking with what looked like a Bible in his hand, and he was closely followed by a figure wearing a winding sheet which the men identified as one of their neighbours. These figures passed by and proceeded into the church, opening and closing the door as they went.

Torpor and ennui evaporated as the watchers, not daring to follow the spectral couple into the church, heard noises they likened to the rattling of bones, followed by the sound of earth being flung into a grave. A few seconds later, the curate, who they hadn't seen entering the church, came out of the door, leading four more figures in shrouds, two of whom they recognised as villagers. The other two were a small child, scarcely more than a toddler, and a stooped and frail-looking old man. As they passed by, the moon came out once more and the ghoulish procession made its way along the churchyard path.

St Vincent's Church, Burton-by-Lincoln.

Understandably shaken by this experience, the watchers headed for home, trying unsuccessfully to put the horrors of the night's events out of their minds. They resolved to keep their observations to themselves.

Within a short time the three people who they recognised had all died, as did a toddler belonging to one of the village women. This left only one other spectre to be accounted for. Soon a relation of one of the watchers who lived in Cheshire sent a messenger with important letters. He was an old man who had the misfortune to undertake the journey during an extremely cold bout of weather. His health suffered severely and, having delivered the letters, he stayed on in the village to recuperate, but died a few days later. The watchers recognised him as the fifth of the grisly spectres they had seen!

Byards Leap

At the intersection of the A17 and the B6403 stands Byards Leap Farm. There are many versions of the legend attached to this locality, but it seems that the local folk were troubled by a witch and they gave the shepherd the job of getting rid of her. The cunning plan was for him to lead some horses out to drink at the pond close to where the aged crone lived. He would then throw a big stone into the pond as the horses drank. Whichever of the horses raised its head first, he was to mount and then call on the witch to climb up behind him. When she was settled, he was to turn round and stab her with the intention that she would fall off the horse into the pond and drown. The first horse to raise its head was a blind one, which was a stroke of luck because no horse with A1 eyesight would let itself come into contact with a ghost.

Everything went according to plan although there was a short delay while the witch finished the tedious task of suckling her familiars. No sooner was she in the saddle than the perfidious shepherd stabbed her. With a scream of agony, the witch fell backwards into the pond, but not before her long, sharp nails had lacerated the shepherd's back. He in turn screamed with agony and the horse, whose name incidentally was Bayard, made a sudden wild leap and landed 60ft away.

This well-known piece of Lincolnshire folklore has, perhaps inevitably, led to people claiming that that they have seen the ghost of a white horse rearing up and making a prodigious leap into the air; always at dusk, if these stories are to be believed. It has to be said that the legend of Byards Leap is only one of many similar stories found in Europe.

The site of the alleged leap is, or was, marked by two sets of four horseshoes, roughly 50yds apart.

Byards Leap.

Cammeringham

Cammeringham is about ten miles north of Lincoln and is little more than a hamlet. About AD 61, Lincolnshire and the eastern counties were being ravaged by conflict between the native Iceni people and the Roman occupying forces. This was all-out war, with quarter neither given nor expected. The Iceni were led by the legendary Boudicca who had scores to settle ever since she and her daughters had been whipped and raped by the Romans.

Boudicca (she was Boadicea when the author was at school) has fascinated generations of school children not only because of her warlike nature, given that she was of the gentle sex, but also because artists' impressions always showed her in a war-chariot with great knives attached to the axles. Any child worth his or her salt was bound to reflect with great relish on the bloody gore that would have resulted from Boudicca getting in among the enemy masses in this horrid war machine with the blades flailing around, lopping off and scattering the Romans' body parts to the four winds. Perhaps at the same time that the 'experts' changed Boadicea into Boudicca, they decided that the idea of the knives on the axles of the chariot were a figment of the Victorian imagination. This killjoy piece of historical revisionism has obviously passed by those people around Cammeringham, who claim to have seen a war chariot pulled by two horses charging out of the early-morning mists, blades swirling from its axles and driven by a fierce-looking Amazon waving a spear.

Culverthorpe Hall

Culverthorpe is a hamlet about five miles south-west of Sleaford. The hall, which is a short distance away, was built in the seventeenth century and remodelled in the eighteenth. In 1730 the owner, Sir Michael Newton, married Margaret, the daughter of a well-connected family from Coningsby. They were a happy couple and the marriage was soon blessed when she gave birth to a fine healthy boy. However, the child died a few months later, apparently killed by the family's pet monkey. This monkey was supposed to

Culverthorpe Hall.

have climbed into the cot, lifted the infant out, carried it to the balcony and hurled it into space, whereupon the poor little wean fell onto the flagstones below, bashing its brains out.

Lady Margaret was devastated by the loss of her child, for which she held herself responsible, believing that she had been negligent in leaving the child alone for a few minutes. She had no more children and was effectively broken by the tragic experience. However, she put a brave face on things and took part in the social round of the gentry in the area. She became known for wearing expensive clothes in a trademark blue. It seems that after her mortal remains were buried, her spirit stayed on in the house, because Culverthorpe Hall is said to be haunted by a 'Blue Lady'.

Digby

This small village is located on the B1188 south-east of Lincoln. In the churchyard there is a rather fine table-tomb marking the burial place of Squire Cook, who died in 1818. Cooke was a noted *bon vivant* and the parties and social events he held were famed far and wide for their food, drink and good cheer. No sooner had the good fellow died and been buried than stories began to circulate that his spirit was continuing with its deceased master's jollifications from within its new abode in the churchyard. The way to arouse the sound of ghostly revelry was to run backwards twelve times around Squire Cooke's tomb.

St Thomas the Martyr Church, Digby.

Doddington Hall

Doddington is a small village a few miles west of Lincoln. The hall was built between 1593 and 1600 by Thomas Taylor, registrar to the Bishops of Lincoln. The architect was Robert Smithson, better-known perhaps for his work at Wollaton Hall in Nottingham and Hardwick Hall in Derbyshire. The building, which is three storeys high and shaped like a letter 'E', is remarkably little-altered today. Doddington Hall is apparently haunted by a ghost known as the 'Brown Lady' who is quite benevolent. She makes it her business to manifest herself if a newly-married woman stays in the house and she apparently gazes rather fondly and reassuringly at them, as if she was herself remembering her own first few blissful days of marriage.

Distinctly more unnerving is the supposed re-enactment of a particularly unsavoury incident in the history of the hall. It is said that a young female servant threw herself to her death from the roof after being pursued around the building by the owner, who was determined to have his wicked way with her. This was in the days when it was regarded as one of the privileges of rank that such men had the right to help themselves sexually to all those women who worked for them. This awful scene is allegedly re-enacted on its anniversary, complete with the appropriate screams as the poor woman plunges towards the ground.

Tom Otter's Lane, Doddington

In 1806, a navvy by the name of Tom Otter had an affair with Mary Kirkham, a girl brought up in the neighbourhood of Doddington. What started out as a bit of honest-to-goodness rumpy-pumpy became complicated when Mary fell pregnant. Also unhelpful in this circumstance was the fact that Otter was married. Since an appalling stigma surrounded the status of being an unmarried mother, as well as that of a child born out of wedlock, all those who knew the couple urged them to get married. Otter did the right thing – to a degree – and married Mary but did the wrong thing by omitting to mention that he was already married. Otter, even though he was not the brightest star in the firmament, must have realised that both wives would legally expect to be kept by him and that he would have responsibility for the maintenance of the forthcoming infant. Anyway, the couple did get married, by which time Otter could already see a great abyss opening up in front of him. He quickly decided that Mary was no longer the love of his life and he murdered her by the side of what is now the B1190. This point near Doddington is now also known as Tom Otter's Lane.

He was soon arrested, charged, tried and, having been found guilty, was sentenced to be hanged and gibbeted. This aggravated punishment meant that his cadaver was hung in chains and displayed at the scene of the crime as an awful warning to passers-by of the wages of sin. It also meant that he was denied the possibility of a Christian burial. Birds pecked out his eyes and consumed the fleshy bits of his body. After a while, all that was left of Tom Otter was a collection of bones in a cage hanging from the gibbet.

It seems that Otter's spirit has always been reluctant to leave the area where he committed the foul deed. In fact, it is supposed to have made itself known soon after the execution and gibbeting, apparently hell-bent on settling accounts with the major prosecution witness on whose evidence he had been convicted. This wretched fellow, John Dunkley, who was actually the local peeping-tom, spent the rest of his life in transports of terror, convinced that Tom Otter's ghost was going to get him.

Otter had bludgeoned Mary to death with a heavy piece of wood and this grisly relic was bought by the landlord of a local pub, the Sun Inn at Saxilby, who felt that putting it on show and telling its story would be a useful way of boosting his trade. He was right. Many people spent a pleasant summer's evening in the Doddington area viewing the gibbet and then repairing to the pub to enjoy gazing at and hearing the bloodcurdling story of the murder weapon. Imagine the astonishment locally when the bludgeon disappeared from the pub on the anniversary of the murder, only to be found propped up against the gibbet and allegedly dripping with fresh blood. The same thing happened on several subsequent anniversaries. All this may sound suspiciously like the landlord trying to boost flagging interest in his prize exhibit, but the ghost of Tom Otter was held responsible for these mysterious movements. Years later, the Bishop of Lincoln, perhaps a trifle unsportingly, decided to put an end to what he clearly thought was superstitious tomfoolery and he had the bludgeon exorcised and then burnt close to the east end of the cathedral.

Even today local folk are reluctant to walk past the site of the gibbet on stormy nights for fear of meeting Tom Otter's ghost. Many who have walked this way say that they have heard the rattling of the chains which held Otter's mortal remains and the creaking of the metal cage which housed them.

Dorrington

Dorrington is a small village strung out along a side road off the B1188 back road from Lincoln to Sleaford. The church of St James and St John has a disproportionately tall tower and an interesting piece of sculpture on the outside wall above the east window. This has clearly been removed from somewhere else and depicts the Last Judgement, with human figures climbing out of their graves and also a representation of the Mouth of Hell.

Over the years, there have been many sightings of an apparently headless man. Some witnesses have said that he carries his head under his arm in time-honoured ghostly fashion, whilst others have said that absolutely no head is visible as this figure staggers around with its arms outstretched. It seems to prefer doing its antics in the vicinity of the village pond and it has also allegedly been seen lurking around the churchyard.

Dunston Pillar

Dunston Pillar stands near to the junction of the A15 and the B1178, a few miles south of Lincoln. It is close to RAF Waddington. This area of Lincoln Heath was a notorious haunt of highwaymen in the eighteenth century. They lurked in the thickets and copses close to the road, waiting with pistols cocked, on their horses ready to accost vulnerable travellers and to persuade them to part with their valuables. It was to counter the threat

St James and St John Church, Dorrington.

Dorrington churchyard.

of these 'gentlemen of the road' that a local landowner, Sir Francis Dashwood (1708-81), who had an estate at Nocton a few miles to the east, paid for what was then called a 'land lighthouse' to be built to as a beacon for travellers coming across the heath. The name Dashwood is not normally associated with public spiritedness because Sir Francis was a notorious rake, the leading light in one of the best-known 'Hell-Fire Clubs', the Knights of St Francis, whose largely rich and aristocratic members engaged in drunken sex orgies, satanic rituals and other libertarian activities. However, perhaps as an example of *noblesse oblige,* Dashwood had what is now known as the Dunston Pillar erected in the 1750s.

The Dunston Pillar.

This curiosity was originally 92ft high and is thought to have supported a coal fire which, at that height, could obviously have been seen from far away across the rural vastness which was Lincoln Heath at the time. Who had the onerous job of keeping the beacon in working order is not known. What is known, however, is that after Dashwood's death, and with a decline in the activities of highwaymen, the beacon was taken down and replaced by a statue of George III. This figure stood gazing out across the Lincolnshire countryside until the Second World War when both the statue and the top 60ft of the supporting column were taken down because they were considered to be a hazard to aircraft from RAF Waddington.

Highwaymen certainly operated in this area and the ghost of one of them, the notorious Dick Turpin, is said to inhabit the area. He has been seen on many occasions on moonlit nights or gloomy winter's days, riding pell-mell across the countryside as though he is trying to evade the clutches of a pursuing posse. Needless to say, this figure is clad in tricorn hat with the required riding boots and cape and astride a magnificent steed answering the description of Black Bess. All this, albeit a splendid idea, is something of a cliché because it is only one of literally hundreds of locations where the ghost of Turpin has been reported. Sadly, Turpin, far from being the handsome, dashing and courteous fellow of popular repute, was actually a small, ugly, pock-marked robber of quite exceptional brutality.

His famous horse, Black Bess, never existed. It was the creation of Harrison Ainsworth, a writer of sensational pseudo-historical novels. If a ghostly highwayman does appear in the area around Dunston Pillar, we can be fairly sure it is not Turpin riding again.

Eagle

Eagle, a small settlement, stands on the by-roads south-west of Lincoln. It seems to be the base for the activities of the particularly unpleasant ghost of a particularly unpleasant man. The man was Charles Murray, who sailed under the command of the buccaneering Sir Francis Drake in the sixteenth century. After he finished with seafaring, and lacking what we would now call useful employment skills, Murray turned to robbery and murder and proved to be a totally pitiless desperado. He ranged around the eastern parts of England in search of plunder and managed to evade the clutches of the authorities for several years. He met his nemesis at Eagle, not at the hand of the forces of law and order but from one of his intended victims who not only fought back, but did so with such effect that he killed his assailant.

A ghost, claimed to be that of Murray, has been spotted from time to time. When it is seen, it always seems to be re-enacting one of the many murders that Murray committed. Those claiming acquaintance with the ghost have described it as engaged in repeatedly plunging a knife into the back of an unseen victim and even accompanying the action with the grunting sounds appropriate to the effort involved. Surprisingly, the invisible victim remains quiet.

Fillingham

This quiet and attractive small village a few miles north of Lincoln is close to the B1398. Fillingham Castle is castellated in a pretty Gothic style and was built in 1760. It has fine views away to the west and two ghosts. One is a 'Green Lady', the other a man who committed suicide and is seen astride a fine white horse.

Glentworth Hall

The B1398 points northwards from Lincoln under the escarpment, with the A15 trunk running along the top. The hall was built in 1566 for Sir Christopher Wray, who was a Lord Chief Justice under Queen Elizabeth I and a signatory to the death warrant of Mary, Queen of Scots. Only fragments of the original building survived into the twentieth century, the rest being more recent work.

From 1760 to 1917 the house was owned by the Lumley family, Earls of Scarborough. It was then sold to a local gentleman farmer. During the Second World War, part of the hall was in use as accommodation for personnel from RAF Hemswell, but after it was severely damaged by a stray German bomb, both the servicemen and the family moved out.

Many of those having associations with the hall mentioned its scary and apparently emotionally-charged atmosphere, although no one ever seems to have heard or seen anything definite. When the war was over, Glentworth Hall had its top storey taken down and the atmosphere changed, everyone agreeing that this action had let the ghosts out. Although the hall became derelict, was it now free of the spirits of the past?

Lincolnshire Black Dogs

Legends of places being haunted by black dogs are common in Britain. These apparitions are solitary, generally about the size of a calf, are shaggy and they have glowing eyes and sometimes, to add to the effect, their slaver is phosphorescent. Probably the most feared of black dogs are those in the northern counties, where they are known as the 'Barguest'.

In Lancashire and Yorkshire, local dialect tends to have them as 'Shriker'. East Anglian versions are known as 'Black Shuck', while Lincolnshire prefers 'Hairy Jack'.

Not surprisingly, these phantom dogs are pretty scary on account of their size and appearance but compared to those elsewhere, Lincolnshire's own Hairy Jack seems to be a comparatively placid, even fairly benevolent, creature. Hairy Jack tends to prefer a rural environment, being at home in the lanes, fields, copses, streams, ponds and boggy areas.

The remote country west of the A15 and north of the A631 around Hemswell seems to be a location favoured by these beasts. People taking their own pet dogs for walks have sometimes become aware that they are being stalked – never a pleasant feeling. The more faint-hearted, having once turned round and ascertained the nature of the stalker, would understandably leg it away from the scene as quickly as possible. Some doughty walkers, however, have reported trying to hit the dog with a stick or throwing something at it. This has proved difficult to achieve because the phantom hound is insubstantial enough for the stick or stone simply to pass through it. The author would prefer the cowardly option.

Dogs are generally reckoned to be very sensitive to the presence of any supernatural entity or force, but those who have been out taking their owners for a walk seem to have been mostly unaware of any uncanny presence.

Metheringham

Metheringham is a large village around the junction of the B1188 and B1189 roads. It is roughly halfway between Lincoln and Sleaford. Its church burnt down in a great fire in 1599, although it has some fabric which dates from before that time. It is of note because it still possesses its very earliest parish registers, dating back to 1538 when Thomas Cromwell ordered that all parishes had to maintain such records. A precursor of the 'surveillance society' of more recent years?

The B1189 is the scene of an oft-repeated supernatural sighting. Innumerable motorists, mainly at night but occasionally during daylight hours, have reported seeing a young woman standing by the roadside and engaged in frantically trying to flag them down. Those who do pull up have claimed that the agitated woman then hysterically declares that there has been a motorbike accident close by involving her boyfriend. She says that she herself is unhurt but her boyfriend is in urgent need of hospital treatment. This woman exudes a not unpleasant smell of lavender, but if the motorist accompanies her to the scene of the crash, the aroma of lavender disconcertingly gives way to the repugnant smell of carrion. Notions of doing one's best to help are being severely tested by this time. Perhaps fortunately, the woman then disappears, as does the smell. There is no evidence of the injured motorcyclist.

This spooky manifestation has been so frequent over the years that she has been nicknamed 'the Metheringham Lass'. The story is that she was a Lincolnshire girl, although a native of Horncastle rather than a local. She became engaged to marry a Flight Sergeant based at RAF Metheringham. Her name was Catherine and it was, in fact, she that died in the accident! The accident itself certainly took place. The couple had been at a local dance when the motorbike skidded on the wet surface. It seems that her spirit cannot bear to part from the scene of the tragedy and that she needs to talk to living people about it and to re-enact the events of that fateful night.

Metheringham Manor House

The Manor House is about a quarter of a mile east of the village and was built late in the seventeenth century. In the 1920s and 1930s there were reports that a ghost was in the habit of spending an hour or two moving furniture about in the middle of the night. Those who claimed to have seen it said that the ghost was black and of an ill-defined shape. One Christmas the Manor was full of guests, two of whom were asleep in a twin-bedded room that was very rarely used. They were woken up suddenly and unpleasantly by a series of loud rapping noises and the apparent creaking of a door. They said that they next saw an 'ungainly black object' with flaming eyes approaching them with an air of infinite menace. When you think about it, anything with flaming eyes coming your way would be a trifle menacing, night-time or not. The 'thing', however, got more than it bargained for. One of the guests was out of his bed in a trice and when the apparition leapt at him, kicked it once and then, for good luck, administered a really hefty whack. Whatever it was clearly could hand out the scares but couldn't take the knocks and it leapt out of the already open window. There was a loud splash, which was odd because there wasn't any water below. Both men, rather repelled by a strong smell of sulphur permeating the room and presumably issuing from the 'thing', then closed the window and got back into bed. With remarkable sang-froid, they were soon fast asleep again.

The next morning, the manor's cat was found drowned in a barrel of water.

Metheringham Manor House.

Nettleham Hall

Nettleham is a few miles out of Lincoln to the north-east and it largely acts as a dormitory village for the city. The hall is over a mile out of the village to the north-west. Much of its fabric was Georgian, but it suffered a severe fire forty or more years ago and was then partly demolished and abandoned. Some of the building remains, an extremely atmospheric and sinister, yet poignant, ruin. The only paranormal story is that of an indistinct shadowy figure in the ruins, believed to be that of a former domestic servant.

The fine iron gates on the lane that passes the site are said to have been made in the early eighteenth century. It is said that they previously guarded the entrance to the churchyard of the demolished church of St Peter-at-Arches in Lincoln. They are as neglected as everything else in the vicinity.

White Hart, Newton-on-Trent

The White Hart is the heraldic symbol of Richard II, a rather nondescript monarch who ascended the throne in 1377 and lost it to a rival in 1399. The village is a few miles north-west of Lincoln and close to the River Trent, which divides Lincolnshire from Nottinghamshire at this point. There is an attractive nineteenth-century toll bridge across the river.

The supernatural activity at the White Hart pub had a lot of publicity in 2004. The licensees, who had been running the pub for about three years, suddenly became subjected to a burst of what was possibly poltergeist activity. The events were disconcerting at best and terrifying at worst. Invisible hands moved tables around and glasses were smashed when unseen hands pulled them off shelves. Possibly worse from the point of

Nettleham Hall gates.

view of customer care, patrons were seemingly spat at by an invisible assailant. Experts reckoned that the phenomena were caused by a local man who, centuries before, had murdered a girl in a building that had stood on the site of the pub. The question as to why this activity should have suddenly broken out in this way remains unanswered.

Nocton Hall

Deep in potato-growing country, Nocton is a few miles south-east of Lincoln. Nocton Hall, built in 1841, was destroyed by fire a few years ago and, ironically, had replaced another house which itself had burned down in 1834. Nocton Hall was the family home of the long-forgotten Frederick John Robinson Goderich (1782-1859). He was appointed Prime Minister in 1827, but he quickly became aware that he cut such a hopeless figure as leader that he was only too happy to resign before he even had time to address the House in his new role. We have had innumerable inept Prime Ministers in the UK, but no others have been appointed and then shown themselves so ready to throw in the towel before going on to enjoy the spoils of office.

The hall had the reputation of being haunted, supposedly by the ghost of a young servant girl who had been raped and then murdered by the owner's son after he had been informed that, very inconveniently, she had become pregnant. The hall had periods of use as an RAF hospital and as a care home. The tragic murder was believed to have happened in one particular room, and staff who slept in this room claimed that they had been woken up on a number of occasions at exactly four-thirty in the morning to find the figure of a young girl standing close to the bed. One of the staff who had this disconcerting experience added that the ghostly girl had been speaking, albeit very incoherently, saying something about the devilish man who had forced himself on her. Other residents and staff mentioned seeing a 'Grey Lady'.

Omens of Death

These items are from a collection of Lincolnshire folklore gathered in the 1840s. They suggest that preparations should be made for an imminent death: if a cock crows at midnight; if when the church bells are being rung, the passing bell is tolled, as if for a funeral; if the sound of a cart draws up at the door but there is nothing to be seen; if a lamp-glass cracks when the lamp is not lit and without it having been struck.

The following may not be fatal, but are tempting fate: to put a lighted lantern on a table; to put new boots on the table; or to open an umbrella in the house before going out in the rain.

RAF Bases in Lincolnshire

There is something undeniably spooky about the surviving relics that can be found on former Second World War RAF bases, of which Lincolnshire has more than its fair share. Perhaps it is something to do with the gaunt and angular appearance of the buildings, many of which were made of concrete. These have developed a patina over the years which has discoloured and perhaps softened them somewhat. Many had austere metal-framed windows. In most cases the glass has long since gone, sometimes along with the frame itself, and this gives them something of a gap-toothed character. The appearance of ivy clinging to these utilitarian structures seems like a silent mock sermon on the transience of human life and the pointlessness of war. The fact is, however, that wars and aircraft and RAF stations were made by humans and these places, full of frenzied activity yet often deep in the countryside, witnessed countless scenes of high drama and the expenditure of prodigious quantities of human emotion. The fear and trepidation wrenching at the gut during the briefing for the next mission; the determination not to reveal your terror in front of anyone else; the elation at returning safely and then the awful realization that your best mate didn't make it. No wonder it has almost become a cliché that where traces of these places can still be seen, they house spooks and spectres. Much has been written about the supernatural aspects of these places and here we will content ourselves with just a couple of stories.

RAF Hemswell was more or less due north of Lincoln on the A15. It has produced ghostly sounds over the years, including the sound of the kind of music that was popular during the Second World War, with occasional bursts of laughter and cheering and the resonating and distinctive sound of the piston-engined aircraft of that era. Seen but not heard is the ghost of a pilot who managed to land his burning aircraft and extricate himself from it, only to die soon afterwards from the severe burns he sustained. Both seen staggering around and heard screaming with agony is the ghost of a member of the base's ground crew who also died from his injuries after his arm was ripped off by moving machinery.

North-east of Market Rasen was RAF Binbrook, from which the famous No.1 Bomber Squadron operated for much of the Second World War. This site is supposedly haunted by a former civilian worker, an Australian, who sympathised with the Germans and agreed to attempt some sabotage at the base. He tried his luck with an Avro Lancaster Bomber, but succeeded only in blowing himself up and thereby suffering injuries which proved fatal. In the years immediately after the war, a figure, alleged to be that of the bungling saboteur, was seen on many occasions pacing restlessly around the perimeter road. Perhaps he is rueing the treasonable activity which, while failing to achieve its objective of blowing up the aircraft, blew him up instead! There were no reported sightings of the ghost of this incompetent fellow for a couple of decades until two men, whose hobby takes them to such former RAF bases and who knew about the story, claim to have seen him, apparently resuming his wanderings.

Riseholme

Riseholme Hall now houses one of the campuses of the University of Lincoln and is about three miles north of the centre of Lincoln.

In the early 1960s, a man who lived near Scampton rode his BSA motorbike into Lincoln and parked it by Brayford Pool. He then met up with his girlfriend, Pat, and the couple went to the cinema – it was warm and a good place for a cuddle. Perhaps there was even a decent film on. When the show was over, they had a short walk and then kissed goodnight, Pat returning home on the bus. The man returned to Brayford Pool only to find, to his intense irritation, that his motorbike had been stolen. He phoned the police

The A15 near Riseholme.

who took the details, but he was left with no alternative other than to trudge home in the darkness. It was a long way and he decided that it was safest to walk along the side of the A15.

It was an extremely cold night and he was glad that he was wearing his thick and long white coat with its collar turned up. He wore thick-soled shoes and so he moved along almost noiselessly. He carried his crash helmet under his arms, with his goggles strapped to the front of it.

Readers who are quick on the uptake will be able to guess what happened next. The man walked along deep in his own thoughts and cursing the unknown person who had stolen his means of transport. There was little traffic at this time of night and he seemed to be surrounded by empty darkness once he got out of the built-up area. He became aware in the immense silence that there seemed to be someone approaching him along the grass verge, coming from the opposite direction. He was suddenly temporarily blinded by the glare from the piercing headlights of an oncoming vehicle. It passed and then he heard what sounded like a choked scream and fast-moving footsteps heading away into the black distance.

The approaching pedestrian had mistaken him for a phantom and the experience gave rise to the story of the 'Riseholme Ghost'.

The Ruskington 'Horror'

In 1998 the television magazine programme *This Morning* broadcast a feature about ghosts. Viewers were asked to phone in with stories of their own experiences. One of those who rang in was the landlord of the Duke of William pub at Leasingham, just outside Sleaford. He told of his frightening experience in the dark early one Sunday morning on the A15 near Ruskington. He was driving along quite quickly when he first of all became aware of a whitish shadow crossing the road ahead. He described it as looking like a white bin liner. Worse was to follow when a sinister-looking face glared in at him through the windscreen for what seemed like an eternity, but it was probably only a few seconds before it disappeared. Over the next few days, dozens of other callers contacted the studio all eager to let it be known that they too had seen something similar on the same stretch of road. What, if anything, lurks on this part of the A15?

A medley of other apparitions has been seen on the A15, which passes about two miles west of the village of Ruskington. They include the ghost of a bus driver, a highwayman and a hermit. How did they know what a hermit looked like?

Saxilby, Woodcocks Inn

Saxilby is a large village which stands a few miles north-west of Lincoln on the A57. It is close to the Fossdyke, built by the Romans to connect the rivers Witham and Trent. William the Conqueror's son later improved the Foss so that larger craft could use it. The pub stands outside the village. A few years ago there were several reports of unexplained activity taking place on the premises. Phenomena have included cold spots, objects being moved around or disappearing completely, vaguely discerned shadows, disembodied voices and a man who, on several occasions, walked up to the pub door and knocked but disappeared into thin air before the door could be opened. When this recurred, the person who answered the knock and was just trying to be helpful felt a right fool and wondered whether he had been hearing and seeing things, or whether there was a prankster about. There have also been reports of the ghost of an elderly woman. Paranormal investigators have not come to any useful conclusions and no phenomena have been reported recently.

Skellingthorpe Church

Skellingthorpe is a village almost due west of Lincoln and it is now becoming a dormitory suburb for the city. In the churchyard attached to the parish church of St Lawrence is a conspicuous table-tomb surrounded by spiked iron railings. This is the resting place of Henry Stone, a local man who was buried in 1693. Just before he died, he requested that his dog be buried as close as possible to him. The dog had saved his life just a few years previously.

He and the dog were taking a walk when a violent electric storm blew up. They took shelter under a large oak tree and the dog became very agitated and kept trying to pull his master away from its vicinity. In the end, he succeeded in doing so, and they had only moved about 20yds when a lightning bolt hit the tree, which exploded in a ball of flame. Had it not been for the dog's action, they would both have been killed. Stone was so grateful that he commissioned a painting in which the dog was shown in a heroic pose. He predeceased the dog but his relations buried the dog close by, as requested. It seems that the dog has remained faithful to its master because many people walking their own dogs past the churchyard in the twilight say that they have seen the figure of a dog amongst the graves. It is said to resemble the dog in the portrait which hangs in nearby Doddington Hall. Attempts to attract the spectral hound by calling or whistling always fail and simply lead to it vanishing in an instant.

Stragglethorpe Hall.

Stragglethorpe Hall

Stragglethorpe is a quiet village about fifteen miles south of Lincoln and close to the A17. The small parish church has features dating from most periods, but is pleasantly untouched by too much restoration.

The hall, which is a mish-mash of architectural styles, is haunted by eerie sounds coming from the attic. These include a noise like hammering on metal and another resembling nothing so much as chains being dragged across the floor. A phantom coach is said to proceed down a nearby lane with the clip-clop of the horses and the sounds of the harness clearly audible.

Temple Bruer

Despite being traversed by the A15 trunk road, the high ground south of Lincoln towards Sleaford is largely lonely and remote countryside. Such names as 'Nocton Heath', 'Dunston Heath' and 'Welbourn Heath' testify to its little-frequented character. What villages there are mostly cluster along the main roads around its outer edges and the A15 itself is remarkable for crossing mile after mile of pleasant, gently rolling countryside with no settlement of any size all the way from Bracebridge Heath to Leasingham, just north of Sleaford.

Standing in this little-known part of Lincolnshire, about two miles west of the A15, is a curious stone tower in the yard of Temple Farm. It can be found at OS TF 009 539 (OS

Landranger 1:50,000 Series). The tower, except for its top, is clearly ancient and is the most visible remnant of a preceptory of the Order of the Knights Templars. This preceptory, in its prime, would have been an impressive establishment with a range of conventual buildings. These would have included a round church, characteristic of the order who designed and built them to be an imitation of the Church of the Holy Sepulchre at Jerusalem. The Templars were inaugurated about 1118 as devout warriors pledged to protect Christian pilgrims journeying to Jerusalem. At first, the members of the order were sworn to poverty, austerity and good works, but over the decades their spirituality degenerated and they became increasingly worldly, amassing large amounts of land and earthly riches. The order was suppressed between 1309 and 1312, by which time their unsaintly conduct had incurred widespread anger and their wealth much jealousy.

Over the years, there have been several alleged sightings in the lanes around Temple Bruer of figures in white mantles emblazoned with a flaming cross, bearing a similar device on their shields while they brandish their swords aloft. They have always been on foot and have only ever been spotted on clear moonlit nights. Are they the ghosts of the Templars of old, returned to, or unable to leave, the scene of their former activities? Are they the visible spirits of these fierce warriors of the long-distant past, men who not so much thought the pen mightier than the sword, but who backed up the Word, as they saw it, with the sword?

This is unquestionably a spooky place on a murky late afternoon in November. There is the splendid old stone farmhouse, probably containing some of the fabric of the domestic buildings of the preceptory, the impressive tower and the almost tangible sense, at least in the right conditions, that the site contains many secrets, by no means all being of this living world.

Temple Bruer.

Horse and Jockey, Waddington

In 2007, the pub had banned smoking, yet the smell of tobacco smoke was often evident. Was the phantom smoker the rather indistinct figure sitting in a far corner that some customers claim to have seen?

Other strange experiences in the pub occurred when, on one occasion, a cleaner had put her mop down for a moment, only to have it thrown at her by an invisible hand. The same cleaner once felt invisible hands stroking her hands and neck. A dark figure has sometimes been seen going into the otherwise empty kitchen, but any of the staff who follow it in report that there is no one to be seen in there.

Joiners Arms, Welbourn

Welbourn is a small village on the A607 road from Lincoln to Grantham, overlooking the low-lying country stretching away to the River Brant and with higher heathland away to the east, towards Ermine Street.

Back in 2002, the chef of the Joiners Arms took the dog out for its customary walk. There was no one in the pub and the chef took care to turn all the lights off before he went. He was amazed, and more than a little disconcerted, when he returned to find all the lights blazing and a CD player blasting out music far louder than normal. The premises were as empty of people as they had been when he had left only half an hour earlier.

This convinced him, previously sceptical about any such ideas, that there was a ghost in the pub. He could not keep his experience to himself and the locals he told were fascinated. They made two suggestions. The first was that the mysterious turner-on of

The Joiners Arms pub, Welbourn.

The sign of the Joiners Arms

lights and CD players was the ghost of a man who had died on the premises some years previously at the notable age of 102. The other suggestion was perhaps a trifle more frivolous. This was that the pub was haunted by the ghost of any one of a number of former regulars who were so devoted to the pub that they spent every possible hour of their life expressing their gratitude for its excellence by doing the only acceptable thing under the circumstances – sitting in the bar, supping and yarning. Whatever put on the lights does not seem to have persisted with such activities, which raises the question as to why it should have chosen to make its presence known on this particular occasion.

Black Bull, Welton

Welton is a growing village, acting as a dormitory for Lincoln, and it stands off the A46 a few miles north-east of the city. There seems to be a natural affinity between pubs and spirits and the Black Bull is well-known as the centre of much supernatural activity. RAF Scampton was nearby, the wartime base of the immortal 'Dam Busters', 617 Squadron. It is therefore not surprising that personnel from the base used the pub and that one of them – a member of aircrew – seemingly returns in spectral form from time to time. Two other visible manifestations are those of a nineteenth-century boy who died while bravely trying to extricate some horses from a burning barn near the pub and a working man of the same century who is supposed to have broken his neck when he fell down some steps nearby.

In the churchyard of St Mary's there is a pile of glacial erratics, large stones gouged out far to the north during the Ice Age and carried southwards in a glacier only to be deposited in the vicinity when the glacier melted and retreated. It has been said that these stones get up and dance around briefly when news breaks of an event that is particularly good for Britain. The last time this happened, or so it is claimed, is when Mrs Thatcher was forced by her Conservative Party colleagues to resign as Prime Minister. Could this claim be nothing more than political propaganda, or 'spin' as it is called these days? Mrs Thatcher always did excite strong feelings of liking or loathing.

GLOSSARY

In the text, the author has used some of the words referring to ghostly phenomena in a somewhat loose fashion. He feels that while this is probably of no great concern to the general reader, it would be useful to provide a simple listing and definition of some relevant terms.

Animal Ghosts

Hauntings involving animals account for a maximum of about 5 per cent of reported ghostly activity. These reports deal almost exclusively with the types of animal with which humans can have an emotional association and/or those that can be put to some kind of use, for example horses, cats and dogs. It is thought that the appearance of some animals, apparently in ghost form, may be a portent of the death of the observer. Related to animal ghosts may be reports of supernatural beasts such as black dogs, and also alleged sightings of such creatures as big feral cats.

Apparitions

Apparitions are the visual appearance of people, animals or things but without their material presence. These manifestations are usually short-lived and they appear, reappear or disappear for reasons that cannot be defined with certainty. Apparitions are only visible to certain people. When they disappear, they do not usually leave any physical evidence. They can apparently move through walls, cast shadows or create a reflection in a mirror.

Some researchers believe that apparitions are a form of hallucination.'Collective apparition' is the name given to those apparitions observed by two or more people simultaneously.

Crossroads

A long-standing belief in folklore is that crossroads attract paranormal activity. Crossroads were frequently used as the burial place for people who had committed suicide. To ensure that its spirit did not wander, a stake was driven through the heart of the suicide victim. It was believed that the conjunction of four roads would confuse the spirit anyway. Crossroad burials were theoretically ended in the UK in 1821, when legislation was passed requiring all churchyards to reserve space for the burial of suicides.

Cyclic Ghosts

These are ghosts that are believed to manifest themselves regularly on specific dates of the year, especially, but not exclusively, on the anniversary of their deaths. Vigils organised by investigators on these occasions do not normally provide the incontrovertible evidence they wish for. In fact, such vigils often involve nothing more than a long, boring and seemingly pointless watch.

Disembodied Voices

These phenomena involve the sound of human voices without any evident human agency. Many reports of hauntings feature disembodied voices. A common feature of this phenomenon is a warning to the listener – which is ignored at the listener's peril.

Exorcism

The idea that an individual can be possessed by a spirit, usually malign, which takes control of him or her, is an ancient one. Exorcism is the practice of a ritual, usually performed by a priest, to drive out this spirit or demon. Many religious groups embrace the idea of exorcism and continue to practice it, albeit to a decreasing extent in the face of growing religious scepticism. Also, many people once thought of as being possessed by demons are now diagnosed as suffering from mental illness.

Ghosts

In the simplest terms, a ghost is the manifestation to the living of the soul or spirit of a deceased human or animal. Some people claim that there are ghosts of inanimate objects such as ships or railway trains.

Ghost Photographs

In its early years, photography was gleefully seized upon by hoaxers and fraudulent mediums to create a stir, to 'prove' the case for the existence of ghosts or to support the case for their own particular powers. Even in more modern times, purported images of ghostly presences or activities are not generally regarded as providing indisputable evidence. Where researchers accept that deception is not intended, accidental double exposures or technical faults with camera or film are often held responsible. A limited number of well-known photographic images, however, have never been totally explained away by supporters or sceptics.

The introduction of digital photography in the 1990s provided a wealth of opportunities to create ghostly images for fun or for the purposes of deception and has only served to make the issue more complicated.

Haunting

Haunting is a word usually applied to a place in which repeated ghost activity allegedly occurs. The nature of the phenomena involved may be visual, aural, olfactory, a combination of these or just a 'presence' sensed in some indefinable way. Hauntings can also involve temperature variations and the unexplained movement of objects. Generally, the impact of these phenomena seems to lessen with time, which suggests that whatever force or energy sustains them gradually dissipates.

Orbs

These are phenomena which only seem to have come to popular attention with the advent, and now widespread use, of digital photography. Orbs appear to be small, often globe-shaped, patches of luminosity not visible to the user of the camera when the picture was taken. While it is claimed by some people that orbs are the souls or spirits of the dead, others argue that they are 'pieces' of concentrated psychic energy. Such paranormal explanations are rejected by those who believe that they are simply airborne particles in suspension which are caught on camera.

Paranormal

A phenomenon which cannot be explained within the existing boundaries of knowledge.